"THE HERO OF MY LIFE"

"*Mag's Diversions*: the first of the trial titles for *David Copperfield*, reproduced from the manuscript, courtesy of the Victoria and Albert Museum, London."

"THE HERO OF MY LIFE":

Essays on Dickens

Bert G. Hornback

Ohio University Press
Athens, London

Library of Congress Cataloging in Publication Data

Hornback, Bert G., 1935-
The hero of my life.

Includes bibliographical references and index.
1. Dickens, Charles, 1812-1870—Criticism and inter-
pretation—Addresses, essays, lectures. I. Title.
PR4588.H55   823'.8   81-565
ISBN 0-8214-0587-X AACR2

for Otto and Sarah Graf

Without the word this universe presents itself to us as what William James called a booming, buzzing confusion; but with that modicum of faith in the word which a child needs in beginning to talk, it soon becomes an orderly, regular, and on the whole comfortable place to live in.

—Lewis Mumford, *My Works and Days,* p. 35.

Just as it takes a certain amount of latent heat to boil water, so it takes energy to "boil" a vacuum, that is, to convert energy into matter.

—Kenneth A. Johnson, "The Bag Model of Quark Confinement," in *Scientific American,* July 1979, p. 115.

"Marcia Massey, you'd better be good. You're going to die some day."
"I am not. I'm going to live all my life."

—Fragment of an overheard conversation, remembered from grade school, c. 1943.

I think I saw the universal form of this complex, because in telling of it I feel my joy expand.

—Dante, *Paradiso* XXXIII (Sinclair Translation).

CONTENTS

References throughout are to the Penguin edition of Dickens's novels. Titles are abbreviated as follows:

PP	*Pickwick Papers*
OT	*Oliver Twist*
NN	*Nicholas Nickleby*
OCS	*The Old Curiosity Shop*
BR	*Barnaby Rudge*
MC	*Martin Chuzzlewit*
DS	*Dombey and Son*
DC	*David Copperfield*
BH	*Bleak House*
HT	*Hard Times*
LD	*Little Dorrit*
TTC	*A Tale of Two Cities*
GE	*Great Expectations*
OMF	*Our Mutual Friend*
ED	*The Mystery of Edwin Drood*
CB	*The Christmas Books*

PREFACE

This book is about Charles Dickens: about the things that he teaches us in his novels, particularly in *David Copperfield*. Because *David Copperfield* is a fictional autobiography—and because the fictional author is a novelist—it is about the act of recollection as an act of imagination. As I read Dickens's works, *David Copperfield* has an especially important place, not because it is in various ways historically autobiographical for Dickens, but because, as he says, he "believed it" so intensely. "The imagination," John Keats wrote, "may be compared to Adam's dream—he awoke and found it truth."[1] Dickens was wide awake, I suspect, all the while he was writing *David Copperfield:* but like Keats's Adam, what he said immediately upon finishing it was that what he had imagined was the truth.

The first five chapters of this book are devoted to *David Copperfield.* For the sake of clarity of focus I have limited references beyond *David Copperfield* to *Pickwick Papers* and *Oliver Twist,* among the early novels. With only minor qualification, most of the comparative arguments contained in these essays could be made with reference to any of the other early novels, through *Dombey and Son.* The last four chapters are on *Our Mutual Friend* and *The Mystery of Edwin Drood*—and again, the choice is one of focus. It isn't that I want to ignore *Bleak House* or *Little Dorrit* or *Great Expectations,* or even *Hard Times* and *A Tale of Two Cities;* but the things I want to say about Dickens and what he teaches us are more fully and obviously demonstrable in *David Copperfield* and the last two novels.

I have not tried to write about everything in *David Copperfield,* even though I have devoted five chapters to my consideration of it. And I have limited even more strictly what I have to say about *Our Mutual Friend* and *Edwin Drood.* I have written, however, about what seems to me the most central and comprehensive theme in all three. The function of the imagination is to know, in that large and generous sense which we call human understanding. Its end is to make us wise. From *David Copperfield* on, Dickens the artist has as his goal the creation of human wisdom. The triumph of his art, perhaps, is in this—and in his ability to make such an ideal the focus of his social criticism as well.

Isaac Newton was a wise man. Had he not been he never would have discovered the law of gravity, which is really the second law of metaphor. To find a metaphor is, as Shelley says, to find "the before unapprehended relations of things."[2] Everything wants to come together, one way or another: even when things seem to be falling apart. Dickens knew that, and let Joe Gargery say it in *Great Expectations:* "Life is made of ever so many partings welded together" (GE, p. 246).

Things do fall apart—naturally—on one level. But on another—and just as naturally—they also come together, become coherent. There is even a mathematical formula which asserts this. What the formula says is that what is lost by way of entropy is compensated for by a gain in information, a gain in the potential for knowledge. I suspect that, long before mathematics or physics were developed—let alone before Lord Kelvin's formulation of the second law of thermodynamics—language was already devoted to the mystery of how things fall apart yet come together.

Language comes into existence when man first senses the separateness of things—that his world is in pieces, apart—and feels the need to make something coherent out of it all: to make of his world a universe. To say the same thing another way, when man realises that he will die, he starts to love—to save himself. Telling himself, desperately, that he will die, he quickly tells the world, "I love you."

David Copperfield is a novel about learning to love the world, and making it by the act of love a universe. It is a novel about how, by learning to love the world, a person—David—can become the hero of his own life.[3] *David Copperfield* taught Dickens more, I suspect, than anything else he ever wrote—and he "believed" every bit of what it taught him. Among other things, it taught him how to write *Our Mutual Friend* and *Edwin Drood.*

If it be alleged against me that in this book I use no single critical method, that I have no properly definable critical focus, I readily admit the charge. The task of the critic is not to develop his own special method or technique—as though a post-structuralist socket-wrench or whatever were the ideal tool to use on everything. Rather, the critic's task is to comprehend as much as he can of a work of art, and to elucidate its beauty and its meaning for his readers. To do this, the critic must use every tool he can handle, every technique of criticism that will assist him toward his end.

There will be other criticisms of this book, and for these also—but in a different way—I must be responsible. For whatever in it might be good, you can thank Dickens, first, and then my friends and teachers and students. Among the latter, the ones to whom I owe the most are Joel Brattin, Jean Carr, Tish O'Dowd Ezekiel, Claudia Gerigk, Don Korobkin, Bill Marcoux, Nancy Metz, and Tony Vogel.

Transcriptions from the manuscripts of Dickens's novels are printed with the kind permission of Mr. Christopher C. Dickens, the Victoria and Albert Museum, London, and the Pierpont Morgan Library, New York. I wish to express my gratitude to the staff of the Library of the Victoria and Albert for the many courtesies and the friendly assistance they have shown me over the past several years, in my work with the manuscripts in the Forster Collection.

Portions of chapter three and the whole of chapter four, in a slightly different form, originally appeared in *Dickens Studies Newsletter* and *Dickens Studies Annual,* respectively, and are reprinted here with permission.

Ann Arbor, Michigan
August, 1980

NOTES

1. Letter to Benjamin Bailey, 22 November 1817.
2. "A Defense of Poetry," paragraph 3.
3. See Walter L. F. Murdoch, *72 Essays* (1947), pp. 147–51.

CHAPTER 1

"This narrative is my written memory."

The full title of *David Copperfield* is "The Personal History, Adventures, Experience, and Observation of David Copperfield the Younger of Blunderstone Rookery, Which He never meant to be Published on any Account." Before settling on this elaborate and complex title, Dickens worked his way through seventeen manuscript slips of trial headings.[1] The rejected titles contain among them all of the elements of the final title, as well as several revealing phrases not in the full title as it appeared on the covers of the monthly numbers of the novel, with Hablot K. Browne's brilliant illustration. An examination of the various elements of those titles, published and rejected, should tell us a great deal about the novel's focus, about Dickens's early understanding of the whole undertaking which we call *David Copperfield,* and about the creative process of writing fictional autobiography. It may even tell us something about Dickens's ambitions as a novelist, which is in part the subject of this book.

The trial titles fall into five significant groups. Three slips record variations on "Mag's Diversions," three more try out "Copperfield's Complete" and "Copperfield's Entire," four call the book something like "The Copperfield Survey of the World as it Rolled," and four are variations on "The Last Will and Testament of David Copperfield." "The Copperfield Disclosures" and "The Copperfield Records" are done once each, and the remaining slip contains the single line—in quotation marks—"Only once a year."

The first slip shows a number of attempts at David's name, and creates as a trial title

"Mag's Diversions."
Being the personal history of
Mr. Thomas Mag the Younger
of Blunderstone House
—"And in short it led to the very Mag's diversions."
And in short they all played Mag's Diversions.
old saying.

The second line is then emended interlinearly to read "Being the personal history, experiences, and observations of," and "Mr. Thomas Mag" becomes "Mr. David Mag"—of "Copperfield House." Dickens doesn't indicate a choice of the "old saying" lines.

The next slip changes the second line to read "Being the personal history, adventures, experience, and observation of" —adding the "adventures" and removing the plural from "experience"—and omits the "old saying" lines. The third version reads: "Mag's Diversions./ Being the personal history, adventures, experience, and observation of/ Mr. David Copperfield the Younger/ And his Great Aunt Margaret."

What is remarkable about the "Mag's Diversions" titles is that Dickens would consider such deprecation of David's work as a novelist as they connote. "Mag" is English slang for a chatterbox, and "Mag's Diversions" are triflings, nonsense.[2] The irony contained in the suggestion of the writer-as-magpie is uncharacteristic of Dickens, to say the least; that he continues the use of "Mag's Diversions" in the third draft of the title, even when David Mag's name has been changed to David Copperfield, is all the more strange. But through its irony, of course, it indicates Dickens's seriousness about his art, and the seriousness of this novel for him, just as much as his calling it "The Artist's Life" or "A Portrait of the Artist" would have.

The fullest of the three versions of the "Copperfield's Entire" title begins with that phrase, but emends it to "Copperfield's Complete." The title continues, then: "Being the whole personal history and experience of/ Mr. David Copperfield/ of Blunderstone House/ which he never intended should be published on any account." "Entire," "Complete," and "whole" are the key words, and they seem to lead directly into the set of titles which call the book "The Copperfield Survey of the World as it Rolled./ Being the personal history, adventures, experience, and observation of/ Mr. David Copperfield the Younger,/ of Blunderstone Rookery./ which he never meant to be published on any account." The ambition toward completeness—the presumption either that the novel could be "Entire," could contain "the *whole* personal history, adventures, experience, and observation" of its hero, or that this character's "personal history, adventures, experience, and observation" could qualify as a "Survey of the World"— is what marks these titles. Though such ambition is not alluded to directly in the final, published title, it is represented graphically in the spinning globe at the center of Browne's illustration, and it is an idea certainly at the center of the novel itself as it is presented to us. These titles are the closest any of the draft titles come to the final version. They are in fact but one title, rewritten three times in almost clean copy, with only such minor changes as the caretting in of "adventures" twice and the dropping of the "Mr." in front of David's name in the third version. By eliminating the first line of this title —but giving it, presumably, to Browne for his illustration— Dickens finds his way to the title we eventually see in print.

I want now to discuss that published title, leaving for a later chapter an analysis of the four "Last Will and Testament" variations and their significance for our understanding of the end of David's novel.

David Copperfield begins with the "personal history" of its hero: "I am Born" is the title of the first chapter. Then, in the next few chapters, as David grows into boyhood at Blunderstone Rookery, his "personal history" modulates into his "adventures." Later, as David leaves his boyhood behind him, his "adventures" in the world become his "experience" of it. Finally, somewhere between chapter 19—"I look about me, and make a Discovery"—and chapter 24—"My first Dissipation"—David's "experience" of the world becomes his "observation" of it. The rest of the novel's sixty-four chapters are given over, then, to his "observation," which becomes in a double sense our observation. What David observes becomes both how we see *David Copperfield* and what we see it as.

The difference between David's "personal history" and his "adventures" is not terribly significant. His "adventures" begin, it seems, when he first leaves home in chapter 3—"I have a Change"—and continue through to his introduction to London in chapter 11—"I begin Life on my own Account, and don't like it." London is "the world," or the big world, or the real world: and David makes perhaps his first critical evaluation of it at this point. His sense of his situation—of being alone in the world, and "without hope" (p. 210)—is heavy upon him, and he feels its injustice. "I led," he says, a "secretly unhappy life; but I led it in [a] lonely, self-reliant manner" (p. 223). And in this life of lonely self-reliance his "character" is "gradually forming all [the] while" (p. 224).

The older David, looking back as he writes, sees himself as beginning at this point to make "his imaginative world out of such strange experiences and sordid things" (p. 225) as London initiates him to. He is forced by his situation into an almost schizophrenic existence. Required to be "self-reliant," treated by Micawber as an equal rather than a child, David conducts himself as an adult in the real world in which he lives and works. He survives, however, as a child, and survives *by* surviving as a child, by keeping his child-self alive in the "imaginative world" he creates out of those "strange experiences and sordid things" (p. 225). His "adventures" in the world—at Murdstone and Grinby's and with the Micawbers, in pawn-shops and public houses—become his painful and unhappy "experience" of it. Similarly, the world he creates in his imagination becomes his "observation" of that real world. The "strange" and "sordid" world hurts young David as he experiences it; but what he observes through his imagination —making "stories for myself," he says, "out of the streets, and out of the men and women" (p. 224)—allows him to learn the world without the hurt or pain. The "little labouring hind" who works at Murdstone and Grinby's (p. 208) is saved by the "innocent romantic boy" (p. 225). The David who was grimly determined to survive in the world by being "self-reliant" discovers in the imagination a safer kind of self-reliance for a child to undertake; and David having found in himself this remarkable capability, Dickens ends his lesson in experience almost as quickly as it began.

David's lesson in experience ends with his resolution to run away to Dover, and his nine day trek to Miss Betsey's cottage. No sooner is he accepted there, however, than he is sent out again to "make another Beginning" (p. 272). But this time David begins as a pupil at Dr. Strong's school rather than as a worker. This time the "experience" of the world will be a more appropriate and congenial one for this "child of excellent abilities" (p. 208); the boy who felt he had been "thrown away" (p. 208) in London, and who feared that he would lose everything he had "learned, thought, and delighted in" (p. 210), will have a chance to learn the world more indirectly now, as a young scholar. This is not to say that David's direct experience of the world is actually over now, though I do want to emphasize that what he lived through in London was a *lesson* in experience. And David sees it as such when he is at Dr. Strong's school: "I was . . . conscious of having passed through scenes of which [the other school-boys] could have no knowledge, and of having acquired experiences foreign to my age, appearance, and condition as one of them" (p. 285).

From this point on in the novel, whatever experience David has is reflexive: simultaneously, now, he both feels the world and registers what he feels as learning. He is already close to living in the way David the narrator later describes his way of writing, as "the blending of experience and imagination" (p. 734).

There is but little space given to David's formal schooling: his career in school at Canterbury takes up only three chapters of the sixty-four in the book. His years at Dr. Strong's are important, however. When he enters the school he is a boy whose knowledge and understanding are still always childishly egotistical, even though he has "acquired experiences foreign to his age": he still sees himself as the center of the world, and he knows only what impinges directly on him. When he leaves Dr. Strong's, he is a young man capable of knowing and understanding things abstractly: everything he sees in the world he can now relate to himself as knowledge. Knowledge thus becomes experience for him: becomes his experience of the world, his growing receptive comprehension of its meaning. The boy who early on "could [only] observe in little pieces" is now a young man capable of "making a net of a number of these pieces" (p. 70), and ready to go out again into the world.

At the end of his stay at Dr. Strong's, in a chapter entitled "I look about me, and make a Discovery," David is asked by Miss Betsey to choose his vocation in life. The "discovery" which David makes while looking about him is not in fact his vocation; that is still some distance in the future. But he does make several other discoveries in this chapter, each related to his progress through life toward that vocation. First he discovers—as an observer, now, not directly involved in the action—that there is something amiss at Dr. Strong's house. Then, toward the end of the chapter, he accidentally encounters his old friend Steerforth—another "discovery"—in a coaching inn in London; and Steerforth, a character out of his boyhood past, appears to David as David sits "filled with the past . . . like a shining transparency, through which I saw my early life moving along" (p. 345).

In an ordinary plot sense it is irrelevant to David's discovery of his vocation that he find out that something is wrong at Dr. Strong's or that he meet Steerforth again. In terms of the plot of David's mind, however, both are important as discoveries in that they represent for us two more stages of progress in David's mental and imaginative development. The trouble between Annie and Dr. Strong is something that happens in the real world, outside of David's self, and he must literally "look about" him to discover this. When he sees Steerforth, however, he sees him—as he always does—more with his imagination than with his eyes. We are perhaps tempted to say that David should be more critical of someone like Steerforth, and more critically responsive to the situation at Dr. Strong's. But the observer cannot act, and the imagination will not judge, however much we may want it otherwise.[3] David the observer's inability to interfere in the scene between Rosa Dartle and Emily is the surest proof of this. If we are to read the *David Copperfield* that Dickens wrote, we must accept the David Dickens gives us; and it is necessary for Dickens's David to learn to observe the real world if he is ever to reach or discover his vocation.

It is David's vocation that makes him special, and demands that we understand him in a special way. What we must learn from David—and from his vocation—is that the imagination can achieve a wisdom that is above judging. The function of imagination is always to recreate, and in recreating the world which it observes it can transform what is in simple reality "strange" and "sordid" into a complex new reality which, if comprehended, is beautiful. Our objection to Steerforth is a legitimate and practical one; but David's response to him is that of an "innocent romantic boy" (p. 225) and a supremely imaginative friend. Neither of these would judge him: the innocent romantic boy could not and the imaginative friend need not. Steerforth creates his own judgment—judges himself—as his friend David the artist creates and remembers him.

As David grows through his life from adventurer and experiencer to observer and finally to imaginer, we discover that what is important about him is the way he sees the world. His vocation, when he finds it, will be that of the artist; and *David Copperfield* is a novel about his progress through his life toward that vocation. In chapter 19, he is still trying to find his vocation, looking both about him and into his past, curiously, in his search.

The next few chapters of this search are given over to David's stay at Steerforth's house and their visit together to the Peggottys at Yarmouth. In all of the action of these chapters, David plays his new role as observer: he observes Steerforth and his mother and Rosa Dartle; he hears Mr. Omer tell of Emily, and watches Emily and Ham together; he meets Miss Mowcher, whose character he had difficulty understanding; and he observes the scene between Emily and Martha in Peggotty's kitchen. During his stay at Yarmouth David also takes daily walks to Blunderstone. "My occupation in my solitary pilgrimages," he says, "was to recall every yard of the old road as I went along it, and to haunt the old spots, of which I never tired. I haunted them, as my memory had often done, and lingered among them as my younger thoughts had lingered when I was far away" (p. 378).

Although David's memory enables him to "haunt" his past, these places in the present are not his. "There were great changes in my old home," he remarks. What he experiences, then, on these walks, is a combination of memory and observation. He remembers Blunderstone Rookery, and observes that "The ragged nests, so long deserted by the rooks, were gone," and that "half the windows of the house were shut up" (p. 378). He remembers looking out his bedroom window at his father's grave—and observes now "a poor lunatic gentleman . . . always sitting at my little window, looking out into the churchyard" (p. 378).

In chapter 23 David does choose a profession, albeit the wrong one, and begins his training in Doctor's Commons. This is followed by the great comic chapter of David's "first Dissipation," which parodies the idea of "observation" in the drunken young David's dissociated observations of himself. "Somebody was leaning out of my bedroom window," he says —and then he discovers that "It was myself." Next he observes "somebody . . . unsteadily contemplating his features in the looking-glass"—and adds, "That was I too" (p. 421). Then, as the party breaks up, "somebody fell, and rolled down [the stairs]. Somebody else said it was Copperfield. I was angry at that false report, until, finding myself on my back in the passage, I began to think that there might be some foundation to it" (pp. 421–22).

David's real profession is that of artist, of novelist, in which he becomes a professional observer of life. His own life becomes in fact "observation," and all that we see of him is in some sense his observation of the world around him. Much of the later action of this novel does not actually involve David, but is rather observed by him: Mr. Wickfield's decline, Heep's exposure, Dr. Strong's difficulties and their resolution; the break-up of the houseboat and Ham's and Steerforth's deaths; Emily's return, and Rosa Dartle's cruel attack on her which David observes but cannot act to stop. The model prison chapter—"I am shown Two Interesting Penitents"—is also a model "observation" chapter; and the final chapter is "A Last Retrospect," in which David reports from the present his concluding "observation" of this world of his —this world which we call, now, *David Copperfield*.

In the beginning of the novel, however, David the narrator

suggests that we take a slightly different perspective on his "observation," and on his "experience" as well. In one of the earlier trial titles David's "experience" is referred to in the plural, as "experiences"; but only once. In the beginning of chapter 2, David the narrator tells us that his intention is to write from "my own experience of myself" (p. 61), which suggests that we might revise the first section of the title to read, even more fully, "the personal history, adventures, and experience of myself": the "experience of myself" being very different from "my experiences." I suggested earlier that David's "personal history" and "adventures" are his "experience" *in* the world, and that what the title calls his "experience" is his experience *of* the world. I would propose now that experience of the world and "experience of myself" are in fact one experience: that for David the narrator, in the act of writing this book, all experience is subjective.

Because his purpose in the writing of this book is to recollect his own life—toward the end, always, of finding out if he is "the hero of [his] own life"—David's observation of the world never pretends to be objective. He insists always that he is honest, but insists too that his focus is on the observing self. And it is this focus that makes David's experience of himself and his experience of the world one. For Mr. Dick "the world" is "mad as Bedlam" (p. 258); for Mr. Micawber it is "the modern Babylon" (pp. 211, 592). For Miss Betsey the world is on the verge of spontaneous combustion—thus her fear of fire, in London. But David never judges the world; rather, he looks at his own impressions of it. It is as though David knows what the word "world" means, etymologically: the life or age of man, all that one man sees. Thus David's experience is indeed the world.

David's world is made up of what he remembers—what he can comprehend from his past—and what he learns from life around him. Because experience is a learning process for him as well as a sensational or eventful one—because everything for David is dramatically subjective as it comes to him—the past and life around him become similar sources of experience in that they are both other than or separate from David until he connects himself to them. By the time we get to the end of *David Copperfield* we must realise, in the layering of its perspectives, that even David's "personal history" and "adventures" are in fact "experience" for David the narrator: they are the recreated experience from the past, out of which he makes both himself and his world. Again, the subjective operation by which he makes the past and the life around him one is what he calls "the blending of experience and imagination" (p. 734).

Taking all of this one step further, we see the imagination as the eye of David's observation. What David the narrator observes primarily is himself—or, rather, David the character. The novel's second chapter is entitled "I Observe"; and what it is about is David the narrator's observation of himself—his recreative observation of his past—as well as David the character's observation of the world about him. "The first objects that assume a distinct presence before me, as I look far back, into the infancy of my past," the narrator says, are his mother and Peggotty. Another way to say this would be "I remember seeing," or "I see myself seeing." To observe oneself observing the world is like experiencing oneself experiencing the world; and just as David's experience of himself and his experience of the world are one, so too his observation of himself and his observation of the world are one. The world becomes David Copperfield—or *David Copperfield*.

A narrator creates his story. He is, by definition, one who knows, or makes, or makes up: the Greek root for our word is γιγνομαγ, to know, from GNA, to create. David the narrator is the central character in this story, becoming through its narrative progress "the hero of [his] own life" (p. 49). And the focus of his story is on knowing, on the act of narration itself. Autobiography is about the self writing, not about the self written about.

But why "Blunderstone Rookery"? Along with David's being always "the Younger" or "Junior" in the titles, this reference to place calls attention again to David's identity, but in terms of someone other than himself. That David is "the Younger" refers us to his father, in a peculiarly insistent way since ordinarily a man named after his father ceases to be called "the Younger" or "Junior" after his father's death, and

certainly a posthumous child wouldn't be called such. Also,
"Blunderstone Rookery"—the place David is alleged to be-
long to—was so named, we are told, by his father.

Dickens obviously spent a considerable amount of energy
looking for the right name for Blunderstone; though as Miss
Betsey says, "Why Rookery? . . . Cookery would have been
more to the purpose, if [Clara and David's father] had had any
practical ideas of life" (p. 53). There are no rooks, of course;
and Miss Betsey worries throughout the novel about the rookless Rookery.

I have worried about this Rookery business, too, especially
after watching Dickens work the changes on the place-name
in the title from "Blunderstone House" (nine times) to
"Lodge" (three times) to "Cottage" (once) to "Rookery" (the
last four times). And why insist on putting it in the title,
anyway? David doesn't live at the rookless Rookery for long
—is thrown out, in fact, by Murdstone—and when he comes
back later to visit it he finds that even the empty old nests are
all gone, and the house is partially boarded up, and a crazy
man inhabits his old bedroom. In what way, we must ask, is
our hero "of Blunderstone Rookery?" And why?

There are two ways to the answer to this riddle of the
Rookery. One is through an examination of what it is that
David loses in losing his home, and how he overcomes this
loss in his life. The other is through an examination of David's
curiously active sense of his dead father, the unfortunate man
who misnamed the rookless Rookery in the first place. These
two approaches are related, of course: David loses his home
—to Murdstone—because he has lost his father; and his re-
placement of his lost home involves the redemption of his
father's name.

That David is a "posthumous child" is announced in the
sixth paragraph of the novel, and the first instance of the
narrator's double consciousness of himself and himself-the-
rememberer occurs in the sentences immediately following
this announcement: "There is something strange to me, even
now, in the reflection that he never saw me; and something
stranger yet in the shadowy remembrance that I have of my
first childish associations with his white gravestone in the

churchyard" (p. 50). At the end of this first chapter the narrator recurs to his dead father, speaking of his own birth in relation to his father's death. He comes to this life from "the land of dreams and shadows, the tremendous region whence I had so lately travelled"; and the light from the room where he and his mother lie shines out upon the churchyard, "the earthly bourne of all such travellers," and illuminates "the mound above the ash and dust that once was he, without whom I had never been" (p. 60).

The progression of these thoughts is complex and telling. First David remembers thinking, as a child, of his dead father; then he imagines back to his birth, and reminds his remembering, imagining self that all who are born must die; and then he teases himself with the possibility of never having existed, and concludes with the realization of his debt to his father. The thought-progression from the memory of his father's early death (and unfulifilled life) through the acknowledgement that we all must die to the tease of might-not-have-been raises the question, indirectly, of the meaning of life; out of his relationship with his father—which ironically is as yet meaningless—David creates, for himself, an affirmative answer. At the beginning of this chapter David was considering whether he would be the hero of his own life; at its end, a few short pages later, he has radically complicated the idea of being such a hero, and has begun to define that ambition by assuming responsibility for his father and his father's life.

David starts his life in this recollection with even more than his father's life added to his own. He is also responsible—and remarks it in the conclusion to this opening chapter—for Betsey Trotwood Copperfield, who remains "forever in the land of dreams and shadows" (p. 60). And to take on Betsey Trotwood Copperfield—David's "sister"—is to take on Miss Betsey herself, who had planned to relive her own ruined life —"there must be no mistakes in life with *this* Betsey Trotwood!" (p. 55)—through her niece. David's responsibility for his mother is also hinted at, in this first chapter, in her fear that she will die in giving birth to him.

At the outset, David tells us that he is supposed to be "privileged to see ghosts and spirits" (p. 49). During the course of the novel, he never sees his father or Betsey Trotwood Copperfield, except as they haunt his imagination; in the final chapter he introduces "a real living Betsey Trotwood" (p. 947)—and he is himself her father, as his father should have been. Once Murdstone sends him away to school he only sees his mother alive once more, though his memory "brings her back to life" for him: "Can I say of her face . . . that it is gone, when here it comes before me at this instant, as distinct as any face that I may choose to look on in a crowded street?" (p. 74). When Miss Betsey discovers that David is David—a boy—she "vanishe[s] like a discontented fairy," he says, "or like one of those supernatural beings, whom it was popularly supposed I was entitled to see" (p. 60). Miss Betsey proves to be more than a ghost or a fairy when the need arises, but the others—David's father, his mother, and Betsey Trotwood Copperfield—are doomed to be his ghosts, unless he can bring them somehow into the world of reality. It is the heroic task of the practical imagination to make a home for them.

Dickens doesn't call the house David and his family live in at the end of the novel "Blunderstone Rookery"—though in his next novel, "Bleak House" is recreated at the end in the new "Bleak House" that John Jarndyce gives to Esther and Allan. But Esther and Allan are "practical" in a way that is different from David's, and they need a physically real house to live in. In this novel, the physically real Blunderstone Rookery is sold, closed, and ruined; the one David makes to replace it he creates in his life, with his imagination. The ideal of Blunderstone Rookery, as conceived of by his impractical father—"he liked to think that there were rooks about it" (p. 53)—is redeemed and realized as David fulfills his ghost-family's lives in and through his own. By living the way he does—by creating the life he creates for himself—he fills the empty nests, symbolically: he fulfills his father's old dream, satisfies his mother's ghost at last, and gives his "sister" a happy home.

It may seem odd to place so very much emphasis on each of these various elements in the long title of a novel most of us—myself included—usually refer to simply as *David Copperfield.* My argument in answer to the charge is two-fold. First, we only earn the right to call the novel *David Copperfield* after we have read it: then, marvellously, the hero is someone whose life—whose whole world—we hold in our hands. Once we have read the book—or each time that we read the book—David Copperfield becomes *David Copperfield:* and he gets there, through the process that Dickens outlines for us in the full title. Second, every detail in this novel, as in all of Dickens's mature fiction, is important. I suspect that this is more true for David's novel than for any of the others. At any rate, David planned for every detail to be significant, and insists on such as he writes. In the first chapter he plays with the idea, accusing himself of "meandering." He manages to get his narrative started in the second sentence—"To begin my life with the beginning of my life, I record that I was born . . ." (p. 49)—but then he tells the story of his caul and the lady who bought it, who was opposed to "meandering." Then he writes: "Not to meander myself, at present, I will go back to my birth" (p. 50). But immediately he meanders again: "I was born at Blunderstone, in Suffolk, or 'there by,' as they say in Scotland." This little meander is a joke; what it says—and it is David's mind saying it to David, remember, since "he never meant [this] to be published on any account"—is that nothing can possibly be beyond the focus of this history, since the book is, reflexively, an examination of that focus. Thus every detail counts in David's book, and the relation between David and Dickens is strong enough that we should count the details in Dickens's title just as seriously as we do the details in David's book—particularly given the amount of effort Dickens seems to have spent working them out. They tell us a great deal of what Dickens knew about David's book, in terms of its themes and its meaning, before he began to write it.

NOTES

1. Manuscript in the Forster Collection of the Victoria and Albert Museum, London.
2. See the *Oxford English Dictionary*, volume M, pp. 21, 307. (In *Bleak House* Grandfather Smallweed calls his wife a "magpie chatterer.")
3. When things at Dr. Strong's finally have to be straightened out by someone, Dickens has to make Mr. Dick do the work, even though the way he acts is out of character for him in its self-consciousness. Mr. Dick has to do it because David can't.

CHAPTER 2

"Whether I shall turn out to be the hero of my own life ..."

The first sentence of *David Copperfield* is, for me, one of the greatest openings in all literature: "Whether I shall turn out to be the hero of my own life, or whether that station will be held by anybody else, these pages must show." There is an immediate sense of remove about the sentence, both in its sense and in its rhythm. The speaker is floating at some distance from these pages, or from the events these pages will detail. The narrative voice introduces itself to us as a voice, as a mind, as a reflective, recollective, observing consciousness: and it is that voice or mind or consciousness that attracts us.

Yeats could have been thinking of such a voice as this when he spoke of writing "with an emotion which I described to myself as cold."[1] *David Copperfield* is a passionate novel, a novel warm with life, rich in emotion and feeling. It is a novel of "powerful feelings," to use Wordsworth's phrase; but in a way that Wordsworth was hardly thinking of when he wrote his famous definition of poetry, these "powerful feelings" are curiously separate in this novel from the act of "recollection" going on.[2] What is recollected is deeply felt, to be sure; we can attest to that from our experience in reading the novel, and we can also point to Dickens's remark in his preface that "no one can ever believe this Narrative, in the reading, more than I have believed it in the writing" (xii). But at the same time that we recognize—and experience—the deep feeling of the recollections that are *David Copperfield,* we are also quite conscious of the act of recollection itself, of the recollecting mind at work: and it is cold but still intense, almost dispassionate but at the same time energetic and absolutely committed to its creative task.

15

The narrative voice in *David Copperfield* is so special *as a voice* that it becomes both the central character and the most memorable character in the novel. Of course, this is as it should be, since the novel is about David the artist, the recollector, the imaginer, and how he sees the world. All of the wonderful galaxy of characters who populate that world are extras, really: they are in *David Copperfield* as tests for David's imagination, as exemplary substances for him to imagine and comprehend.

David the narrative voice calls attention to himself frequently: and as he is a voice more than a character or person, it is appropriate that he attract our notice not so much by what he says as by how he says it. It is the tone, the rhythm, the feeling of that opening sentence which attracts us, I think, long before the mysterious thing it says begins to sink in. The two long formal clauses introduced by "whether," the first one almost entirely monosyllabic, are followed by the heavy falling cadence of "these pages must show." If you scanned the sentence, it would look like this:

Whether I shall turn out to be the hero of my own life, or whether

that station will be held by anybody else, these pages must show.

That is not an arhythmical prose sentence; it is, rather, a remarkable creation of a rhythm.[3] It will reappear several times during the course of the novel, as the form of a certain kind of rhetoric, a voice. The rhetoric is the rhetoric of reverie, of "retrospect"; the rhythm calls attention to the abstracted imagination that is doing the musing and recollecting and reviewing. It calls us back from the story to the storyteller: from the narrative to the narrative voice.

The question asked in the opening sentence—whether David will be the hero of his own life or not—is difficult on the first level because ordinarily we presume ourselves to be the heroes of our own lives, and thus we do not even hear such a question. True, I have my heroes—like Ted Williams, or Dickens, or my father; but they are *my heroes,* not the heroes *of my life.* I expect to be the hero of my life—automatically. But in his abstracted state as an imaginer and a voice, David be-

gins by questioning this. He poses the question, however, not
as David the character, or even as David the narrator (who is
after all a character too in some way). He asks the question
as the narrative voice: so that the question becomes, then,
whether the imagination—abstracted, noumenal, looking at
its phenomenal world—can become substantial and heroic. If
David is to be "the hero of [his] own life," then the book *David
Copperfield* must become the life and imagination its hero.How
"these pages" can "show" this, can prove it, will be by creating a real phenomenal world for us, as readers, and by
demonstrating the imagination's comprehension of that
world.

The key, again, is comprehension. I am reminded of Dostoyevsky's *Crime and Punishment,* which in my translation is full
of the word "understanding."[4] Raskolnikov wants to "understand" it all, and everybody else in the novel wants him to as
well. Dostoyevsky—so much influenced by Dickens, and so
much taken by both *David Copperfield* and *Great Expectations*—
started the Raskolnikov part of the novel as a first-person
narrative. It went badly, of course, because Raskolnikov *does
not* understand it all, which is why he has a fever. Much of the
time he is—or has been—delirious, because he cannot comprehend Petersburg, cannot comprehend the world. For Dostoyevsky as well as for Dickens, the resolution of the world's
madness is comprehension, understanding. David's comprehension of the world satisfies us at the end of his novel. We
are satisfied not with the world, but with him. The conclusion
of *Crime and Punishment,* however, offers us a very different
experience: it is Dostoyevsky who "understands," not his
hero. Raskolnikov understands the symbol for comprehensive acceptance of the world—kissing the earth in the Hay-
market—but he may not in fact believe in what the symbol
represents or be truly converted. Dostoyevsky is not con-
vinced, certainly, that his hero believes what he should believe
or that he understands enough to be saved. That is why he
tacks on the Epilogue, and runs Rodya through everything—
from alienation and fever to Sonia and relief—again, and tells
us then that he is saved. But the Epilogue is not very satisfac-

tory. What comes through most strongly for us as readers is Raskolnikov's need to understand, and it is in this need that we identify with him.

Raskolnikov and David are certainly far apart as characters, but they do share that need to know, to understand it all; and sharing it makes them almost brothers. Raskolnikov is actually more like Mr. Dick than David. Like Dick, he knows the world is mad, but cannot comprehend it; its madness is bigger and more complex than his mind. He is confused by his experience and observation of life and in such a state commits the murders which almost destroy him. For David, however, the need to understand is not dangerous. Petersburg fever does not become his fever; the world's madness does not make him mad. His experience of the world is imaginative, his observation of it an artist's observation. And from his imagination of the world, David creates himself. Edward Wasiolek, the editor of the notebooks for *Crime and Punishment,* quotes Dostoyevsky's final determination that "the story must be narrated by the author and not by the hero," and continues, "In this way the action is given to the hero, and the consciousness and significance of the experience are given to the author."[5] In *David Copperfield,* the action is given to the other characters, and the consciousness and significance of the experience are given to the author—to David the narrator—*as* his heroism. Point of view creates the hero as he comprehends the world which "these pages . . . show."

It takes David nearly a third of the first chapter of his novel to get to its opening scene, on the day of his birth. More than anything else, the opening several pages serve to establish the self-consciousness of the narrator as a narrator and as a narrative voice, recollecting. He sets up the different sources of his narrative very carefully, scrupulously indicating to us how he knows what he knows. "I was born (as I have been informed and believe) on a Friday" (p. 49) is an example of one kind of information, that which he receives at secondhand about himself. "I was present myself [at the raffle sale of my caul], and I remember to have felt quite uncomfortable. . . . [It] was won, I recollect, by an old lady" is another: it is his report of his own memory. A third kind of information—and the most important—comes from David's pulling his memory of the past up into the present. It creates, in effect, that other dimension of this novel, the "story" of the narrative voice itself. "There is something strange to me, even now," David writes, "in the reflection that [my father] never saw me; and something stranger yet in the shadowy remembrance that I have of my first childish associations with his white gravestone in the churchyard" (p. 50). This and other "shadowy" memories are really what *David Copperfield* is about, at its deepest level.

At the beginning of Chapter 2 David writes of his earliest memory, of his mother and Peggotty as "the first objects that assume a distinct presence before me, as I look back, into the blank of my infancy" (p. 61). He remembers them so particularly—his mother as all that she ever is, "with her pretty hair and youthful shape," and Peggotty "with no shape at all, and eyes so dark that they seemed to darken their whole neighborhood in her face, and cheeks and arms so hard and red that I wondered the birds didn't peck her in preference to apples." He even remembers "the touch of Peggotty's forefinger as she used to hold it out to me . . . roughened by needle-work, like a pocket nutmeg-grater"—and then he defends himself for the detail of this memory:

> This may be fancy, though I think the memory of most of us can go farther back into such times than many of us suppose; just as I believe the power of observation in numbers of very young children to be quite wonderful for its closeness and accuracy. Indeed, I think that most grown men who are remarkable in this respect, may with greater propriety be said not to have lost the faculty, than to have acquired it; the rather, as I generally observe such men to retain a certain freshness, and gentleness, and capacity of being pleased, which are also an inheritance which they have preserved from their childhood. (61).

The "power of observation" that David speaks of here is the same thing that Coleridge praises in trying to define Wordsworth's "genius";[6] and David's claim for himself here is very close to what Coleridge claimed for his fellow poet. The continuance of this power, David says, marks a man's character with "a certain freshness, and gentleness, and capacity of being pleased"; and these virtues become, for Dickens, the virtues upon which he would build heroic life. Clearly this "power of observation" is—literally—a power: it is observation empowered by imagination to govern action.

Late in the novel David speaks of his method of writing as "the blending of experience and imagination" (p. 734), and this is also what he has presented from the beginning as the method of his life. His closely observed past experience is what David remembers; and he finds—or creates—the meaning of these memories in the present through the power of his imagination. Thus this novel has its most significant meaning, finally, in the present from which and toward which the past is recollected. The meaning of *David Copperfield* is in the creation of David's heroic life: the life which becomes heroic as it achieves meaning and happiness.

The way the imagination creates happiness is perhaps more difficult to explain than the way it creates meaning, primarily because we do not usually think of happiness as being such a serious thing as it is for Dickens here. Throughout his career, Dickens seems to have thought of happiness and meaning as being different aspects of the same thing. If *meaning* is created when spirit informs matter, then *happiness* is created by the physical embodiment of spirit; that is, as meaning comes from the imagination's comprehension of the world of its experience, so happiness comes from the experience itself *as it is* comprehended. It is not simply that one is the life of the mind and the other the life of the body. Rather, meaning knows experience, and happiness is the phenomenal form or expression of what is known. In their "ideal" state, for Dickens, they are almost identical, as meaning represents wholeness and happiness is fullness.

Meaning is a word that belongs for the most part with the reflective, recollective point of view in *David Copperfield;* and for most of the novel happiness is a word that is used in relation to characters and experiences. The narrator David often focuses attention on his happiness or unhappiness, weighing and understanding his experience accordingly. Miss Betsey hopes that the young David will grow up "happy and useful," and those words appear together, then, over and over again. Agnes is "happy and useful"; David wants to become so. In the final chapter—entitled "A Last Retrospect"

—David reviews his world in terms of the happiness achieved by its various inhabitants. Curiously, he does not tell us about his own happiness, directly. But in the last sentence of the preface which he wrote immediately after finishing *David Copperfield,* Dickens remarks that writing this novel has "made me happy"; and that statement, taken at its most serious value, can be read as David's as well as Dickens's.

It is easier to demonstrate how the writing of *David Copperfield* has made David useful than how it has made him happy. Late in the novel, as he and Agnes talk together about his work as a writer, she tells him: "Your growing reputation and success enlarge your power of doing good" (p. 915). And Mr. Micawber writes to him from Port Middlebay: "Go on, my dear sir, in your Eagle course! The inhabitants of Port Middlebay may at least aspire to watch it, with delight, with entertainment, with instruction!" (p. 945). The "power of doing good" is the power of the social critic, the teacher. Dickens has been a social critic, frequently but incidentally, in all of the novels before *David Copperfield,* and in the novels which follow this one he creates whole fictions which are criticisms of society. He has written and will continue to write novels which instruct as well as entertain, teach as well as delight. Dickens must be aware of the reference to the traditional function of art in Micawber's praise of David's writing; and the claim which this praise makes for David's art must be as seriously intentional as it is obvious. *David Copperfield,* however, is not itself just a novel of social criticism—or not such a novel in the way Dickens's other works are. The most important thing *David Copperfield* teaches us is David's life: his heroic life of comprehension.

Wordsworth ends *The Prelude* proposing "that the history of a Poet's mind/ Is labour not unworthy of regard," and that this history has a high didactic value:

> what we have loved,
> Others will love, and we will teach them how;
> Instruct them how the mind of man becomes
> A thousand times more beautiful than the earth
> On which he dwells.[7]

David never makes a claim like this for himself or his work, directly: but the way the narrative voice insists that we focus our attention on David the mind tells us that Dickens has made an assumption much like Wordsworth's about the didactic value of "the history of a Poet's mind"—or a "Portrait of the Artist." Thus not only is David's writing this novel the most "useful" thing he ever does for himself, it is also the most useful thing he could ever do for us. This novel has made him the hero of his own life—and it has made that heroic self a model for Dickens and for us.

David is a model which no one—Dickens or us—ever lives up to, and in this he is unreal: "ideal," to use Coleridge's word. He has it all together, to use today's vernacular—and that echoes Coleridge's other word for what the imagination does, "unify." Art teaches and delights, traditionally; and as we all know, it doesn't teach us either to do anything or not to do anything. It teaches us itself: it teaches us what it is. Dickens is almost always a bad—heavy-handed, sentimental, even hypocritical—moralist; but he is a wonderful metaphysician. And here, because everything about this novel—everything about Dickens's creation of it—comes under the idealizing influence of David's successful attempt at heroism, there is almost none of that kind of moralizing social criticism that preaches against and punishes evil or rewards the good. The closest it comes to that is in Agnes's "hope," expressed in response to Heep, "that simple love and truth will be strong in the end . . . that real love and truth are stronger in the end than any evil or misfortune in the world" (p. 372), and David's remark to Uriah after his exposure, near the end of the novel: "It may be profitable to you to reflect, in future, that there never were greed and cunning in the world yet, that did not do too much, and over-reach themselves. It is as certain as death" (p. 829). But neither of these remarks is, finally, a moralizing one. Agnes does not ask for "the principle of Good surviving through every adverse circumstance, and triumphing at last" (OT p. 33); she hopes, rather, that love and truth may be strong enough for us to build our lives on them, even in the midst of evil and misfortune. David's remark goes beyond this, to argue the essence of evil. Evil punishes itself, he tells Uriah, threateningly: it *is* its own punishment, just as he is his. Conversely, goodness is its own reward. Goodness comes from happiness, and is rewarded with happiness, naturally—and that, too, is "as certain as death."[8]

The clearest articulation of the metaphysical state of happiness in all of Dickens's works is in *A Christmas Carol.* When Scrooge goes out, after his conversion, into Christmas day, he finds that his change has changed the world. He becomes, Dickens says, "as good a friend, as good a master, and as good a man, as the good old city knew, or any other good old city, town, or borough, in the good old world" (CB, I, p. 134). It is as though Scrooge's new goodness is contagious, and Dickens can't stop writing the word; and the reason for this is that Scrooge has found, upon looking at the world this new morning, "that everything could yield him pleasure" (CB, I p. 131).[9]

Much more substantially than Scrooge, David achieves a perspective from which he can view the world with pleasure. Of course, this achievement requires a metaphysical conversion on David's part, too; the "trial by adversity" motif that runs all through Dickens's work quite literally requires of David—twice—that he recreate himself. The first time is after his mother's death, the second after Dora's. The self he recreates after Dora's death, through his experience of near despair and mystical regeneration in the Alps, is the artist-self who writes this novel. It is a self that has overcome, through sympathy, the selfish ego which feels and registers pain only as pain; and free now from that ego, that *person,* David becomes his selfless understanding of the world. The voice that narrates this novel for us comes into existence in Switzerland when, under the influence of "great Nature," David is reborn.

What happens to David in the Alps will be examined in detail in Chapter 5; for now I want to keep to the theme of David's heroic self. In tracing that theme we have come to the climax: the new self which comes into being in Switzerland will be the hero of David's life. Almost immediately upon his conversion, David sets out "to get a better understanding of [him]self" (p. 890). To do this, he will reflect upon and recollect his past, recreating his life through the combined power of memory and imagination. Though he recalls sad things, they will bring him understanding now, not sorrow. Imaginative comprehension supersedes sorrow and pain. It is a pleasure of the soul: and David, who before "had had no purpose, no sustaining soul within [him]" (p. 887), has now a new soul. And the soul, for Dickens, has the greatest "capacity for being pleased" (p. 61) that we know. When the soul of a man is happy, Dickens says, "everything [can] yield him pleasure." And if everything yields pleasure, then life is full, positively whole, and "ideal."

In this world we live in—that Dickens lived in—only the imagination, the soul, can create ideal life. The miracle of *David Copperfield* is that, as we finish the novel, we *believe* this ideal life—just as Dickens did. "No one," he wrote, "can ever believe this Narrative, in the reading, more then I have believed it in the writing" (p. 47). But as we move away from the novel, and consider more carefully—more objectively—what David's achievement really is, we begin to qualify our appreciation of it, perhaps. And we begin to ask questions—Keatsian questions—about what is real here, the story or the storyteller? And what makes the storyteller a hero? Does memory only remember, or is imaginative recollection a substantial and real recreation of life? Is life only fully life when it is understood, when it is comprehended by the imagination? Is the highest human pleasure truly in such comprehension? And is that pleasure wisdom?

At several points in the novel David stops to remind us that this book is a remembering. He speaks of his "life" as a "volume," and of time and events that "will never pass out of my memory" (p. 168), of "days" that "occupy the place of years in my remembrance" (p. 169). Things from the past, he says, "are things not of many years ago, in my mind, but of the present instant" (p. 209). Sometimes he stops to wind his memory up: "Let me remember how it used to be," he writes, introducing a typical scene at Blunderstone, "and bring one morning back again" (p. 103). Chapter 18 is entitled "A Retrospect," chapters 43 and 53 "Another Retrospect," and chapter 64 "A Last Retrospect."[10] The language and imagery with which Dickens introduces these chapters are as interesting as the reason for their being set in such a format—and the two are related. The first retrospect is introduced this way: "My school-days! The silent gliding on of my existence—the unseen, unfelt progress of my life—from childhood up to youth! Let me think, as I look back upon that water, now a dry channel overgrown with leaves, whether there are any marks along its course, by which I can remember how it ran" (p. 322). The reflecting, retrospecting mind looks at its past sympathetically but objectively, and recognizes that it was life unconsciously experienced: "the unseen, unfelt progress of my life." The recollection of that life, in the present, is a "silent" reproduction of "unseen, unfelt progress." The past is dead—"now a dry channel overgrown with leaves"—and yet through the imagination it can be turned again to "flowing water." Importantly, then, the David who watches this re-created stream of life not only recreates it as life—as a dramatic scene for us—but also observes it critically, to discover "whether there are any marks along its course, by which I can remember how it ran." Again, though the novel is made enjoyable for us as a dramatic experience by David's vivid and detailed re-creation of the past, the introductions to this and the other retrospect chapters show clearly that the past is important to David only as it influences the present. Miss Betsey has once advised him, "It's in vain, Trot, to recall the past, unless it works some influence upon the present" (p. 407); and this idea controls the novel.

Chapter 43 begins: "Once again, let me pause upon a memorable period of my life. Let me stand aside, to see the phantoms of those days go by me, accompanying the shadow of myself, in dim procession" (p. 691). The real character is the present character of David, the voice that we are listening to, the mind's eye viewing the past for itself and revealing that past to us. "Let *me* stand aside," it says, to see the past as "phantoms" and the past self as but a "shadow." The chapter ends with a repetition of this incantatory introduction: "I have stood aside to see the phantoms of those days go by me. They are gone, and I resume the journey of my story" (p. 700). The spell is broken, and the novel returns to a more normal narrative mode. The self-consciousness relaxes—but the focus of the novel, which is closely linked to that self-consciousness, remains unchanged: the narrator resumes, not his story or his journey through life, but "the journey of [his] story"—as though his story were itself a character.

The third retrospect—chapter 53—is the chapter in which Dora dies. It is the shortest chapter in the novel. Rhetorically, it is the most intense. It begins: "I must pause yet once again. O, my child-wife, there is a figure in the moving crowd before my memory, quiet and still, saying in its innocent love and childish beauty, Stop to think of me—turn to look upon the Little Blossom, as it flutters to the ground!" (p. 834) The first sentence stops us just as it does David. It is an unwilling stop —"I must pause"—and the unwillingness is underlined, almost dramatized in the sound and sense of "yet once again." There is a "moving crowd before [his] memory," but it moves separately from David the narrator at the very beginning of the chapter. His pause here is one of intense consciousness, and the few short pages which follow will record not a progress of events so much as a sequence of emotional responses toward a climax. At the end of the chapter, when Dora has died, the remembered character David will be stopped, too—at the point of numbing emotional crisis which David the narrator already feels in his memory at the beginning of this retrospect: "It is over. Darkness comes before my eyes; and, for a time, all things are blotted from my remembrance" (768). In the interim between that first stop and this last, the narrator calls up the past into his present, and makes that brief last day of Dora's life exist again in his mind: "It is morning. . . . It is evening. . . . It is night. . . . It is over" (pp. 834–839).

What differentiates these retrospect chapters from the rest of the novel is their style—and their style, of course, indicates what is really different about them, the special relation between the narrative voice and its subject matter. As I have argued earlier, the focus of *David Copperfield* is on David's remembering, not on what he remembers. In the retrospect chapters what we see is memory enacted: a direct, dramatic representation of the act of remembering. The retrospects are all written in the present tense, and their scenes are more like tableaux than dramatic scenes. They have the quality of theatrical illusions, as though they are presented through a scrim. At one point, under the influence of an evening at the theater, David describes his meditation on the past in just such terms, as appearing "like a shining transparency, through which I saw my earlier life move along" (p. 395). Later, in writing about his purpose in this novel, he revises the scrim figure so that the emphasis is on the illuminating eye rather than what is illuminated or that illumination itself. His intention, he says, is "to reflect my mind on this paper" (p. 765). *David Copperfield* is the mind of its hero reflected on a screen, superimposed on the images of plot, character, and action. Or, to use the tableau metaphor again, this novel is the reflection of David's mind on the scene itself. The most intense examples of such reflection are the retrospects, in which David freezes the action, in effect, in order to recover and dramatize what the action felt like to him in its time. The experience of these chapters is the narrator's direct and conscious reexperience of feeling, of what he felt when he first experienced the action or event. Thus in those formal "It is morning. . . . It is evening. . . . It is night. . . . It is over" divisions of chapter 53, the antecedent of "it" is not really time, but feeling.

Though these retrospect chapters re-create feeling—are moving, emotionally intense chapters to read—they are still very different in their effect from other dramatic narratives. Again I think of Yeats' "emotion which I described to myself as cold" as a way of explaining the difference. The cause, I am sure, lies in the kind of appeal these retrospects make to us. Their appeal—their projected communication—is from mind to mind: from David's mind, experiencing emotion, to our minds. We are unaccustomed still to the mind's communication of feeling *as* feeling, comprehended. And it is difficult for us to accept the "ideal" comprehending David—David the narrator—as real.

David's mind presents itself to us in these retrospect chapters as that disembodied voice which spoke the novel's opening sentence. The purpose of that voice, or mind, is to create meaning and pleasure out of its life, its world, and through its power of recollection—re-collection, really—make that life or world full and whole. The final chapter of the novel, "A Last Retrospect" exists as a retrospect in part just to claim that purpose achieved. It begins:

> And now my written story ends. I look back, once more—for the last time—before I close these leaves.
> I see myself, with Agnes at my side, journeying along the road of life. I see our children and our friends around us; and I hear the roar of many voices, not indifferent to me as I travel on.
> What faces are the most distinct to me in the fleeting crowd? Lo, these; all turning to me as I ask my thoughts the question! (946)

This has been the "written story" of David's life. David himself is the center of attention: *I see me,* he says, *in my life, and I hear voices talking to me and about me as I go by.* The third paragraph of this introduction seems to change the focus to those voices, those "faces" in the "the fleeting crowd" around him. Actually, however, David the narrator's question is whom among the crowd *he* sees most clearly in *his thoughts:* "What faces are the most distinct to me . . . turning to me as I ask my thoughts the question." He presents them: Miss Betsey, Peggotty, Mr. Dick, Mrs. Steerforth and Rosa, Julia Mills, Jack Maldon, Dr. Strong and Mrs. Markleham, and then Traddles. Except for Traddles, with whom there is a short scene to be played, they are all presented in tableau. Then "these faces fade away. . . . shadows which I now dismiss"— and it is over.

What is left? David, and David's mind. What is real? Again, only David, and David's mind. The rest is shadow. It existed only in David's mind, as the substance of his imagination; it exists now only as this novel, called by David's name: *David Copperfield.* The ambition "to reflect my mind on this paper" (p. 765) has been fulfilled; and "these pages," which must identify "the hero of my life," identify him by means of his reflection as a life, a world, called *David Copperfield.*

NOTES

1. *The Autobiography of William Butler Yeats* (New York: Collier Books, 1965), p. 48.

2. "Poetry is the spontaneous overflow of powerful feelings; it takes its origin from emotion recollected in tranquility." Wordsworth, "Preface" to *Lyrical Ballads,* 1800 edition.

3. In the manuscript, this line originally reads "Whether I shall turn out to be the hero of my own life, or whether that position will be filled by somebody else...." The substitution of "station" for "position" and "anybody" for "somebody" helps keep an accentual rhythm from developing.

4. The Russian word used throughout by Dostoievski is *ponyeemath* or *ponyath;* its root is a member of the "take" or "hold fast" family of words, from the Sanskrit YAMATI.

5. *The Notebooks for Crime and Punishment* (Chicago: University of Chicago Press, 1967), pp. 9–10.

6. *Biographia Literaria,* chapter 4 (Modern Library edition), p. 155.

7. *The Prelude,* book 14, lines 413–14, 446–450.

8. Cf. *Our Mutual Friend* for Dickens's formulaic representation of this idea: "And oh, there are days in this life, worth life and worth death. And oh, what a bright old song it is, that oh, 'tis love, 'tis love, 'tis love, that makes the world go round!" (p. 738).

9. Dickens seems originally to have conceived the sentence about Scrooge to read something like "He became as good a master, as good a friend, as good a man, as any old city knew." As he writes it, however, the line expands, building itself upon repetitions of the word "good": "He became as good a [master] friend, as good a [friend] master, as good a man, as [any] the good old city knew, or any [old] other good old city, town, or borough, in the good old world" (Ms. 65). The manuscript is in the Pierpont Morgan Library, New York.

10. Though not designated a retrospect in its title, Chapter 33—a chapter full of Dora and David and Julia Mills and the Desert of Saraha—ends: "Of all the times of mine that Time has in his grip, there is none that in one retrospect I can smile at half so much, and think of half so kindly" (p. 490).

CHAPTER 3

"I could observe, in little pieces ... "

"Somebody's sharp," Mr. Murdstone warns his friend
Quinion. David thinks Murdstone means him, but is "relieved
to find that it was only Brooks of Sheffield" (p. 72). Immediately before this scene David fails to "understand" (p. 70)
Murdstone's flatteries of his mother; and though he knows he
dislikes the man, he cannot find a "reason for it"—"certainly
... not *the* reason that I might have found if I had been older"
(p. 70).

Not knowing is dangerous; not being able to comprehend
things, by "making a net of a number of ... pieces" (p. 70)
is frustrating, and often causes injury or loss or pain. Though
David the narrator claims once to prefer "the simple confidence of a child" to "worldly wisdom" (p. 120), his narrative
documents profusely the usefulness of wisdom and the disas-
ter that often comes from misplaced confidence or simple
ignorance. The range of examples, in David's case, runs from
Murdstone's stealing his mother and Brooks of Sheffield's
innocence through his "blind" (pp. 565, 582), infatuated love
for Dora. When David begins to see his mistake in marriage,
he is haunted by Annie Strong's words about "the first mis-
taken impulse of an undisciplined heart" (p. 733); and when
as the narrator David thinks of his ignorance of Agnes's love
for him, he laments "if I had known then, what I knew long
afterwards!" (p. 582).

According to Clara Copperfield, David's father believed
"that a loving heart was better and stronger than wisdom,"
and had thus "borne with her," and was made "a happy man"
by her love (p. 186). When David and Dora are trying to find
their happiness, David has to give up trying to "form [his]

little wife's mind" (p. 764). He has been "trying to be wise," he says (p. 763)—and trying "to make [Dora] wise too" (p. 764), which is what causes the trouble. David agrees to give up his efforts to change her: "You can never show better than as your own natural self," he tells her. Dora interprets this as "It's better for me to be stupid than uncomfortable" (p. 764), but David corrects her: "Better to be naturally Dora than anything else in the world"(p. 765).

Because David loves Dora—"I love her dearly as she is" (p.764)—he will quit trying to change her; but because he knows the value of wisdom, he rejects stupidity as in any way a good thing. He finds that affection by itself can't make them "happy," for all their promises to each other, and "the old unhappy feeling pervaded [his] life" (p. 765). Dora may be a repetition of David's simple, loving mother, but David is determined not to be a repetition of his naive and ineffectual father: David wants to "improve the world a little" (p. 540), even as a young man—and he is already certain that improvement doesn't come from ignorance or stupidity or even innocent good will.

David is always interested in knowing, as a child and as a man. David the narrator remembers himself as "a child of close observation" (p. 61), "a child of excellent abilities . . . with strong powers of observation, quick, eager" (p. 208), and full of "wondering" (p. 121). He is susceptible to "apprehension and dismay"—even "fever"—when he doesn't know or can't understand things (p. 124). As a man, David sets out as courageously as anyone pursuing knowledge ever has, to know himself and the world he lives in.

As a child, David does his lessons with his mother, and then with the Murdstones. Next he is sent to Salem House, "a school carried on by sheer cruelty" where the boys "were too much troubled and knocked about to learn" (p. 146). David's most important teacher during these years, however, is Peggotty. She teaches mostly—entirely—by example, and except that he learns his letters from his mother, he learns all of the important things from Peggotty. She teaches him what love is, and how to love. She teaches him loyalty, too, and selflessness and honor: all the long virtues of life. She also teaches him how to learn his own life, and how to tell himself his story.

"Peggotty's narration" (p. 186) to David of his mother's death contains two curious—and crucial—interruptions. On both occasions Peggotty stops speaking, and beats softly upon David's hand. Then she continues "in her way," to tell him "all that she had to tell concerning what had happened" (p. 185).

Peggotty begins her narration with Clara's weakness before her baby is born, and goes on to describe how, in her weakness, "she got to be more timid, and more frightened-like," so that "a hard word was like a blow to her":

> "But she was always the same to me. She never changed to her foolish Peggotty, didn't my sweet girl."
> Here Peggotty stopped, and softly beat upon my hand a little while.
> "The last time that I saw her like her old self, was the night when you came home, my dear. . . . " (185)

The second interruption comes in the midst of Peggotty's telling David of his mother's last night alive:

> "On the last night, in the evening, she kissed me, and said: 'If my baby should die too, Peggotty, please let them lay him in my arms, and bury us together. . . . Let my dearest boy [i.e., David] go with us to our resting place,' she said, 'and tell him that his mother, when she lay here, blessed him not once, but a thousand times.' "
> Another silence followed this, and another gentle beating on my hand.
> "It was pretty far into the night," said Peggotty, "when she asked me for some drink. . . . " (186)

The first interruption comes at a crisis of remembering for Peggotty. Taking care of Clara Copperfield has not been easy for her, because of David's mother's willfulness and capriciousness; but Peggotty loves her—has loved her—and puts up with her. So the point is not that David's mother has "never changed . . . to Peggotty," but that she has always been difficult to Peggotty, has always been weak in character, in moral courage and fortitude. Because she has been so weak, she has been easy for the Murdstones to manipulate and change—and Peggotty and David both know this, have known it since their first night back at Blunderstone after Clara's

marriage to Mr. Murdstone. That evening, when David is sent
to bed, Peggotty follows him, to soothe his sorrows. Then
Clara comes, and calls David a "naughty boy" for crying and
Peggotty a "savage creature" for comforting him (p. 94). David the narrator describes her manner as "pettish and wilful"
as she laments that this is a "troublesome world" (p. 95).
Then, when Mr. Murdstone comes in and stops her "pouting"
with a whisper and a kiss, David says of himself: "I knew as
well that he could mould her pliant nature into any form he
chose, as I know, now, that he did it" (p. 95).

When Peggotty tells David that every "hard word" was
"like a blow" to his mother, and follows that with the assertion that "she was always the same to me," and then beats
softly upon David's hand, her silent tapping says what doesn't
need to be said out loud: that Peggotty never turned on David's mother, never hit her or hurt her, and that she won't do
so now by saying anything bad about her. In the manuscript,
Peggotty first "stopped, and smoothed my hand," as though
her purpose were to help the truth of what she has just said
to sink in. When the gesture is changed, so that she "softly
beat upon my hand a little while" (Ms. 111), its meaning
changes. Her beating on his hand continues her narration
without words, and says the deeper and painful truths about
Clara which Peggotty won't say aloud. David seems to understand this—at least David the narrator does, and like Peggotty
refuses to say anything directly critical of his mother. They
both know, of course, that she deserted them for Murdstone,
but they still love her, and love doesn't criticize unnecessarily.
To talk of Clara's having changed, now that she is dead, would
be worthless, useless, to both Peggotty and David.

The second interruption—"another silence . . . and another gentle beating on my hand"—comes after Peggotty has
told David his mother's parting words for him: Clara had
wanted him to accompany her funeral procession, and had
wanted to "tell him that his mother, when she lay here,
blessed him . . . a thousand times." Those blessings are not
worth much to David—and he and Peggotty know that, too,
and agree to it without having to say anything. Again, it won't
do anybody any good to comment or complain, so Peggotty

doesn't. But David needs to know it—to know it with Peggotty —so she tells him, in code.

In the manuscript, this second interruption is introduced several times as though unconnected with the first interruption: "She here . . . ," "Peggotty stopped for a while . . . ," "Peggotty stopped here and. . . . " Then Dickens creates her stopping as of a pair with her previous gesture: "Another silence followed this, and another gentle beating on my hand" (Ms. 111). The false starts indicate Dickens's careful concern with both the form and the meaning of Peggotty's narration. When he connects this second pause back with Peggotty's earlier stopping through the gesture of her "beating on [his] hand," he has found the meaning and completed the form.

David learns something about how to tell himself his story from the way Peggotty manages "in her way" to tell him "all that she had to tell" (p. 185). Like "Peggotty's narration" (p. 186), David's way of telling his story to himself does its criticism silently. David the narrator's indirect judgement of his father's disvaluing "wisdom" (p. 186) is one example of such silent criticism or correction. Another example also has its beginning here, in what Clara asks of David as she dies. When we compare her requests with Dora's, at her death, we see what David is telling himself about the difference between the two.

Clara is a self-pitying, sentimental fool, and what she asks for as she dies—that David "go with [her and her new child] to our resting place" is both self-indulgent and doubly—trebly—morbid; her "blessing him . . . a thousand times" is pious and self-serving. When Dora is about to die, however, she apologises to David for having been "too young" to be married, "a silly little creature . . . not fit to be a wife" (p. 837), and assures him that "it is much better as it is" (p. 838) with her dying now. Then she sends him away, and speaks alone to Agnes. Later, we find out that Dora's "last request" and "last charge" were that Agnes would someday marry David (p. 939). Dora is a much wiser young woman than Clara Copperfield ever was—and a much more generous one. Quietly, without ever saying anything about it, David teaches himself this by means of the details he recalls about their deaths.[1] He doesn't need to assert the specific differences between them, to judge them so overtly and explicitly. We know what the differences are—and David does, too. Constantly and consistently aware of meaning in terms of understanding or comprehension, David makes this act of autobiography a cumulative act of imaginative organization, a "net" of meaning woven in the mind. In reading this novel, I never worry that David doesn't put the things together that I put together: rather, I worry always that I am missing connections and intricate organizations that his imagination comprehends.

David's measures of his father and mother are made by reference to his own belief in wisdom and Dora's wise generosity. His way of teaching himself these lessons—of making himself know and understand without indulging in useless and destructive criticism of the dead past—is copied from Peggotty's quiet, charitable way of telling them both in her "narration," "all that she had to tell."

Again, "narrative" itself is a kind of knowing, from the Greek word γιγνομαι; and like knowing, narration is a creative act, a bringing into being. The roots of the word tell us, too, that narration is a feeling or emotional or physical kind of knowing—"womanly" or "motherly," in fact, through γεινομαι—rather than abstract knowledge. By definition, narrative is not about ideas, but life: about knowing and learning life.

David Copperfield is insistently a novel whose theme is knowing and learning. On one level this theme is created out of the idea of schools and schooling: after his years of lessons at home and his two terms at Salem House, David goes on to Dr. Strong's school, and then becomes an articled clerk in Doctor's Commons, to learn that profession. On another level, the theme of knowing and learning is established and elaborated by such references to knowledge—or ignorance—as I have mentioned above, and by a number of similar references, scattered promiscuously throughout the novel, which serve to define its focus. David tries to "form [Dora's] mind" (p. 764), and teaches himself shorthand (pp. 608 ff.). The Heeps extract information from David (p. 314). Dr. Strong, whom Mr. Dick respects for his "wisdom and knowledge" (p. 310), spends his life working on a dictionary. Miss Betsey, having learned her lesson from the world, takes young women "into her service expressly to educate [them] in a renounce-ment of mankind" (p. 250). Mr. Wickfield is forever wanting to know the "motive" for everything. Agnes helps David with his studies when they are children, and later keeps a school for girls. Miss Mowcher, "as shrewdly and sharply observant as anyone" (p. 395), reads Steerforth's mind: "If I understand any noodle in the world," she tells him, "I understand yours" (p. 394). One of Rosa Dartle's several distinctive gestures is her saying, over and over, "But is it really? I want to know" (pp. 350 ff.).

It is David, however, who most needs to know things—because he needs to know the world, and understand it. And when he goes to bed at night, after meeting Rosa for the first time, he finds himself obsessively mimicking her obsessive question—"Is it really, though? I want to know" (p. 356)—in his dreams.

Some of the references to learning are more important in the novel than others, because they reflect directly on David's way of learning. Rosa's question, Dr. Strong's dictionary, Mr. Wickfield's motive-seeking are all identifying characteristics, gestures which through their repetition call attention to the individual personality. And as it is David the narrator who emphasizes these tics by his repeated memory of them, they become signs of his understanding of the characters: they⁻ become his way of identifying them. Uriah's writhing, Mr. Micawber's letter-writing, Peggotty's work box with the pink dome of St. Paul's on the lid, Mr. Dick and King Charles's head, Miss Betsey's hatred of donkeys, Traddles's skeletons, etc.—all of these are emblems which David creates to mark character and personality. To test the accuracy of each of these as a representation of a particular character and person-ality, David recurs to it each time he meets the person. As the novel draws to a close, David begins to collect these gestures, as proof, in a sense, of his understanding. Thus the last time we see Uriah, in the model prison, he greets David "with the old writhe" (p. 924). Mr. Micawber last appears, appropri-ately, by letter (pp. 945–46). Peggotty appears in "The Last Retrospect" with all of her usual paraphenalia, including "a work box with a picture of St. Paul's upon the lid" (p. 947); and Mr. Dick is "making giant kites"—but they are plain kites now, not plastered over with King Charles's head—and he will "finish the Memorial when [he has] nothing else to do" (p. 947). Near the end, when David is back in Dover with Miss Betsey, he notes that his aunt "allowed my horse on the forbidden ground, but had not at all relented as to the donkeys" (p. 932). When David sees Traddles on his return from Switzerland, he asks Tommy about "skeletons," and his old friend admits that he still draws them: "I am afraid there's a skeleton —in a wig—on the ledge of the desk" (p. 920).

Knowing—and that includes, certainly, knowing the people around you—is always important in Dickens's world, and particularly so for David. Dickens was such an acute observer that he readily identified significant "peculiarities and oddities" (PP, p. 45) in people, and from such signs came to an accurate understanding of them. In the 1847 preface to *Pickwick Papers* Dickens defends this method of observation and characterization, arguing that all of us begin our knowledge of a character with impressions of his "peculiarities and oddities," and then, as we become "better acquainted with him . . . begin to look below those superficial traits, and to know the better part of him." What is remarkable about Dickens's art, of course, is that in creating a character like Mr. Pickwick, Dickens's insight is so acute that his impressions of those "peculiarities and oddities" prove to be fully reliable and accurate representations of "the better part of him."[2]

Looking at "peculiarities and oddities" first may be the way we all begin our acquaintances with each other; but few of us have the eye for such revealing detail that Dickens has, and on first meeting we rarely succeed in discovering each other's essential selves through some physical or linguistic tic or gesture. Dickens makes these discoveries regularly, novel after novel: so much so that it becomes one of *his* characteristics, a signature for his work. One of the languages in which he writes—from *Pickwick Papers* through *Edwin Drood*—is the symbolic one of gesture.

Dickens wrote his 1847 defense of Mr. Pickwick in response to a complaint about the "decided change" in that character through the course of his novel.[3] The manuscript of this preface makes it clear that Dickens knew, obviously, what his defense of Mr. Pickwick was, but he had trouble finding the right way to say it—perhaps because he had never before bothered to ask himself exactly how he created characters. He starts by arguing that no readers will find the change in Pickwick "forced or unnatural . . . if they will reflect that in real life the peculiarities and oddities of a man who has anything whimsical"—and then he stops. "Anything whimsical" doesn't seem quite it, so he crosses it out—and then writes it back in, and continues. The whole paragraph looks like this in the manuscript:

> It has been observed of Mr. Pickwick that there is a decided [difference] change
> [change]ʌin his character, as these pages proceed, and that he
>
> becomes [more good and] more [wise] good and sensible. I do
>   forced or
> not think this change will appearʌunnatural to my readers, if they
>   in real life
> will [reflect back that unless it] reflect thatʌthe [oddnesses] pecu-
>
> liarities and oddities of a man who has [anything whimsical] any-
>
> thing whimsical about him, [are] generally [the first means]
>   [only a very] [only a little]
> impress us first, and that it isʌ[only when we know him on a]
>   are
> [more substantial] not until weʌ[know him] better acquainted with
>   superficial traits, and
> him that we usually begin to look below theseʌ[and to] [appear-
>   to know [him more and better] the better   part of him
> ances and respect him for less superficial reasons].[4]

The end is to "know" the character, "to know him as he is," and finally "to know the better part of him." The gesture— the peculiarity or oddity become symbol—takes us inside the character. As it is used in *Pickwick Papers,* the technique is a simple one, and perhaps it is wrong to speak of it as symbolic in any serious way. In later novels, however, this method of characterization becomes much more sophisticated and complex, and truly symbolic. In *David Copperfield,* David borrows the technique, and makes it his way of "knowing" people.

David introduces Miss Murdstone as a dark, perversely masculine creature with heavy eyebrows. A Freudian critic would need little more than this to fix Miss Murdstone's character accurately. But the definition of Jane Murdstone that such analysis gives us does not fully represent her character; and though Dickens's descriptions of his characters frequently include the details necessary for our making accurate psychological analyses of them, his major characters are always more than psychological types, and their special gestures usually signify something larger and more meaningful than simple psychological traits. In Miss Murdstone's case, neither her masculinity nor her eyebrows—which she has grown, David tells us, to compensate for her lack of a beard —become her gesture. Instead, Dickens creates and elaborates a richer, more complex, more individual, and more eccentric symbol for her, which begins as her luggage and proceeds through her purse to her decoration to her person.

In the manuscript of *David Copperfield,* Dickens creates Jane Murdstone very carefully. The paragraph which introduces her looks like this:

                             [very dark sour] gloomy-
    It was Miss Murdstone who was arrived, and a[very dark, ugly]
              whom she greatly resembled both in face and voice
  looking [woman she] lady she was—dark, like her brother, and
                nearly meeting over her [long] long nose
  with [solemn] heavy eyebrows as if [not] being disabled by the
          wrongs   had carried them
  [fragility] of her sex from wearing whiskers she [had made the
            to that account. [She brought] She brought with her two
  most of them and did not] [?] uncompromising hard black boxes

  with [her] her initials on the lids in hard [?] brass [nails] nails [and]
          her money out of a hard [steel] and she kept the purse
  When she paid the coachman she took [a] steel purse [which she
        in a very jail   bag
  kept jam full] of [?] a [? ? hard steel ?] which hung upon her arm
                     heavy chain [?]   [? ?]
  by a [perfect little clasp fastener] and shut up like a bite. I [hated

  her quite] had never, at that time, seen such a metallic [person]
  lady, altogether,
  as Miss Murdstone was. (Ms. 53)

What has caught Dickens's imagination is the metal symbol. Miss Murdstone's eyebrows are psychologically telling—like Betsey Trotwood's linen and her "gentleman's gold watch." Dickens, however, is rarely satisfied with creating his characters psychologically and identifying their psychological motivations for us. Mr. Wickfield depends on "motive" as a way to understand things, and it is obvious that Dickens finds both the method and the understanding unsatisfactory. He insists on knowing more than simply why his characters act as they do; he wants to know who they are. He wants to know them metaphysically as well as psychologically, and his way to the metaphysical is through symbol, or symbolic gesture.[5] Thus, for example, more important than the details which show and explain Miss Betsey's masculinity are her marvellous aversion to donkeys and her heroic protection of that "patch of green" in front of her house at Dover. From these two bits of information we discover Miss Betsey's state of being as well as her state of mind: she has retreated from the large world, where she was hurt, to a small fortress which she defends against all intruders. The donkeys and the green place are symbolic, for Miss Betsey; her gesture is to protect the green place from those beasts; and what the gesture represents is her metaphysical state of retreat and defense.[6]

The language of gesture discovers a character's essential identity by representing dramatically the cause or source of that identity: gesture thus becomes what one *is*, not just what one *does*. In creating Miss Betsey, Dickens began with the exposition of her past in the opening chapter. His note for this exposition, in the first number plan for the novel, is simply "Miss Betsey—Her old wrongs." But when she is about to re-enter the novel, in chapter 13, Dickens conceives of her in dramatic and symbolic terms, and his notes to himself are for gesture rather than exposition: "Miss Betsey— 'Janet! Donkies!' " and "Donkies/Miss Murdstone comes on a donkey."[7] Just as Dickens creates Miss Betsey out of these brief phrases which identify her gesture, so we discover her character—her metaphysical character—through her gesture. And it is through our understanding of her character that we make sense of those psychologically telling details of her rather masculine dress and that large gold watch.

Similarly, what really creates the character of Jane Murdstone is the symbolic representation of her "metallic" nature rather than the psychologically accurate and useful description of her masculine aspect. Further, Dickens's elaboration of her character through this gesture shows us not only how Dickens creates her character, metaphysically, but for whom he creates it as well. The perspective which sees everything through the language of gesture—which comes "to know the better part" of a character through his "perculiarities and oddities"—is the artist's perspective, not the analyst's. The artist wants "to know"—to comprehend—"the better part" of every man. Both Dickens and David, as artists, need to "know" the world: for them art is a creative and philosophical fascination with life, with the dramatic enactment of being. The story of David's novel demonstrates this in its account of Jane Murdstone and how David comes to know her. In his relationship with her—and it is a relationship because he makes it such!—we can see quite clearly how the creation, comprehension, and expression of a character's self or "better part" becomes, for the artist, an end in itself.

David is fascinated by Jane Murdstone's symbolic identity, so much so that, though her room is "a place of awe and dread" for him, he cannot resist peeping into it when she is absent. What he notices there are "numerous little steel fetters and rivets, with which Miss Murdstone embellished herself when she was dressed, generally hung upon the looking glass in formidable array" (p. 98). At first, in the manuscript, David discovers "all sorts of little fetters and fastenings;" then "fastenings" become "rivets" and the "little fetters" become "little steel fetters." He sees these bits of metal on Miss Murdstone when she is dressed;[8] seeing them here on her mirror —in the polished metal or leaded glass before which she sits to decorate herself—he sees her, in effect, reflected in them.

David continues to see Miss Murdstone in terms of her gesture. When she pretends to cry, David tells us that she "made a jail-delivery of her pocket-handkerchief, and held it before her eyes" (p. 100). When we see her in the parlor, she isn't knitting or crocheting, but sits "stringing steel beads" instead (p. 103). And when David comes home from school for the holidays, he identifies Miss Murdstone by reference to her "metallic" self immediately. Dickens first writes her response to David's salutation on this occasion as " 'Ah dear me!' replied Miss Murdstone, giving me her forefinger." Then he makes her simple reply into a sigh, and reintroduces her gesture: "her forefinger" is deleted, and she gives David "the tea-caddy scoop instead of her fingers" (Ms. 100). If we read this revision as a sort of plot-metaphor it tells us—accurately, truly—that she has extended herself and her control in the house. But if we read it as the substitution of a gesture-reference for ordinary description, which seems to me more appropriate and also more rewarding, we see the power of Dickens's—and David's—focus on the metaphysical, essential character of this woman.

One of Dickens's frequent tricks is the dehumanization of characters. In *Bleak House* Grandfather Smallweed is a pillow that needs punching up. Pancks, in *Little Dorrit,* is a tug boat. Both Sir Leicester Dedlock and Lord Decimus Tite-Barnacle are "magnificent refrigerators." Wemmick, in *Great Expectations,* has a post-box mouth. In *Our Mutual Friend* Silas Wegg not only has a wooden leg, but seems to be in the process of growing another one. Most of these examples are static; the gesture or symbol is either used once in passing or recurs unchanged and unchanging. But the dehumanization of Jane Murdstone is both elaborately and subtly progressive. She begins, in chapter 4, thanks to her accoutrements and their metaphoric relation to her, as a "metallic lady." By the time we get to chapter 8 and the substitution of the tea-caddy scoop for her fingers, her relation to things metal has progressed from the metaphorical to the physical: from *rivets and fetters are like the lady* to *tea-caddy scoop and fingers are interchangeable!*[9] In chapter 9 David comes home for his mother's funeral, and must see Miss Murdstone again. The tone is solemn now, and neither David the child nor David the adult narrator can see the "metallic lady" with wonder or humor. Though Jane Murdstone is one of the child David's terrors

she also strikes his imagination, and is a wonderful vision for
him as well as a terror. As the adult David looks back at her
and at his childhood comprehension of her, he is in part
amused; and because of this we laugh at her perversity more
than we loathe or fear it. But when David's mother dies there
is no room for amusement or wonder, and Dickens's representation of Jane Murdstone has to change.

What happens is one of the brilliant things in Dickens. At
first he presents her "busy at her writing desk, which was
covered with letters and papers" as David enters. Then David
tells us that she "gave me her index finger, and asked me if
I had been measured for my mourning." Then the "index
finger" is cancelled in the manuscript, and with a caret Dickens substitutes her "cold finger-nails." To further reinforce
the symbolic suggestion he also revises "[she] asked me if I
had been measured for my mourning" to read "[she] asked
me in an iron whisper . . . " (Ms. 109/p. 182). The gesture is
still there, though hidden. Or, rather, it is not hidden—because symbols don't hide meaning, they create it. What has
happened is that the gesture is no longer just a gesture. Jane
Murdstone has become her gesture, metaphysically. She began, through David's comparing her to her rivets and chains,
as a "metallic lady": a metal-modified lady. Now she *is* metal,
with her "finger*nails*" and that iron whisper of a voice.[10]

Miss Murdstone's character is proved now, and though she
makes three more apprearances in the novel, her metallic
gesture is not developed beyond this point. She is given a new
gesture, briefly, in the next chapter, one that judges her,
comically. While David is still being kept at Blunderstone
after his mother's death—and worried about not being back
at school—he is "idle," according to Miss Murdstone (p. 189).
But David is not too idle to be watching her character. She
accuses David of idleness while "looking into a pickle-jar" (p.
189)—in which dark vat she sees, of course, her own pickle-
puss reflection. She stays there, "still keeping her eye on the
pickles" for a moment, and then looks at David "out of the
pickle-jar, with as great an access of sourness as if her black
eyes had absorbed its contents" (p. 190). Just as she is metaphysically "metal," so she becomes "pickle."

In the manuscript, Dickens introduces Miss Murdstone's "looking into a pickle jar" interlinearly, as an after-thought, and as she continues her remarks to David, Dickens has to interrupt her speech in order to repeat the gesture:

"Humph!" said Miss Murdstone, ["It is of more]ₐ still keeping her ₐeye on the pickles, [and thoughtfully]ₐit is of more importance

than. . . . " (Ms. 115)

The final reference to the pickles, which makes the metaphysical connection between their "sourness" and hers, is clear and unrevised in the manuscript: which says, I think, that once Dickens found the gesture he knew what it meant.

Miss Murdstone appears next in chapter 14, when she and her brother call on Miss Betsey at Dover. There is not a single reference to her metallic gesture in this scene, nor is she given any other special kind of identification. What she says is introduced with simple "she said" tags, and Miss Betsey refuses to recognize her existence. At her last appearance—in chapter 26, when she is presented as Dora's "confidential friend"— she is much subdued. When she meets David she touches his hand "with the tips of her cold, stiff fingers," and arranges "the little fetters on her wrists and around her neck"; and these, David says, "seemed to be the same set, in exactly the same state, as when I had seen her last" (p. 453). She has not changed—naturally! And then he tells us: "These remind me, in reference to Miss Murdstone's nature, of the fetters over a jail door; suggesting on the outside, to all beholders, what was to be expected within." This last sentence, with its reference to the metallic lady's "nature" and its assertion of the relation of surface to essence, is added in the manuscript, seemingly in Dickens's rereading of the whole page—heavily reworked—on which it appears (Ms. 280). Beyond this, the references to Miss Murdstone's "fetters" in chapter 26 are ironic and even *dis*connected from her. The chapter is entitled "I fall into Captivity"; and when Dora talks about not liking Miss Murdstone and wanting to choose her own friends, David hears her "every word" as "a new heap of

fetters, riveted above the last" (p. 456). David's borrowing
her gesture for reference to himself is at one level a warning
to us of the naivete of his love for Dora at this point, and a
symbolic or associative foreshadowing, perhaps, of his later
Murdstone-like attempts to mold her character. More positively—and more directly—his comic use of her "fetters" here
is his way of showing us that Jane Murdstone's "nature," now
that he comprehends it with his imagination, is no longer in
any way dangerous to him.

Uriah Heep is created in much the same way as Jane Murdstone is. His character is simple, finally, though in his representation of it in psychological terms Dickens gives us so
many examples both of symptom and of cause or source that
it seems complex. Uriah's role in the novel is simple, too, in
a plot sense: he is the villain. David, however, isn't interested
in the plot—we are none of us, surely, very interested in the
plots of our lives!—and as this is his novel, his interest must
govern and direct ours. David is interested in Uriah as a type
of person whom he must learn to deal with, whose being he
must imagine and comprehend.

Heep is not just repulsive to David; like the terrible Miss
Murdstone, he is also attractive to David's curiosity. When
David first sees him, what he remarks is a "bony" creature
with "a cadavorous face" and "a long, lank skeleton hand" to
match, "which particularly attracted my attention" (p. 275).
Uriah has red hair "cropped as close as the closest stubble,"
"hardly any eyebrows, and no eyelashes" for his "red-brown"
eyes—all of which stimulate David into "wondering" about
him. What seem to be Uriah's gestures are quickly obvious at
this first meeting: he "writhes," and is " 'umble." His writhing
is meant to express pleasure, and ironically it does. His
humility is of course false. Uriah feigns pleasure at meeting
Betsey Trotwood and David, just as he feigns humility before
them. In this false " 'umbleness" we see his cunning, his ambition, his greed, his pride. When he writhes with pleasure we
see first that the pleasure is only pretence—he is *not* in fact
glad to see Miss Betsey or David—and second that he takes
real and perverse pleasure in being false to them, in having
the chance to act a lie to them. It is this latter aspect of Uriah's

character that makes him so fully evil. Unlike Fagin in *Oliver Twist* or Daniel Quilp in *The Old Curiosity Shop*—in their different ways his two most important predecessors—Uriah is always and uncompromisingly evil, and always seriously so.[11] He is not just a caricature, or a humour character, or even just a villain. He is an essentially evil person; and in a novel the theme and method of which are both concerned with David's comprehension of the whole world—as "Copperfield's Entire"—such a character becomes extremely important. In *Nicholas Nickleby* Dickens speaks of "the world" as "a conventional phrase which . . . often signifieth all the rascals in it" (p. 20); here he gives to the world's chief rascal, as the revealing symbol of his identity and his most significant gesture, the wonderful name "Heep."

The brilliance of Uriah's name is perhaps enough to make us understand the gesture. Late in the novel, however, Mr. Micawber, with his great enthusiasm for words, is given the honor of explicating "Heep" as a gesture, and then, at the end of the scene, David speaks his understanding of its meaning in a single pithy sentence. Toward the end of chapter 49 Micawber invokes "Mount Vesuvius" dramatically, and promises to have soon "blown to fragments . . . HEEP!" (p. 779). He discovers in himself "a smouldering volcano long suppressed" (p. 781), and prepares us thus for chapter 52, which is entitled "I assist at an Explosion." Miss Betsey tells Micawber that she is "ready for Mount Vesuvius," and he promises that she "will shortly witness an eruption" (p. 812). But the eruption is not just—or even—in Micawber, or in his energy; what is exploded is Heep. And whereas the linguistic discovery of Jane Murdstone's metallic essence is subdued by the mood of the scene in which it occurs, the language is given fireworks and capitals here, and the metaphoric and metaphysical identifications explode at us. Asked "What is the matter?" by David, Micawber replies with a rich dramatic pun:

> "What is the matter, gentlemen? What is *not* the matter? Villainy is the matter; baseness is the matter; deception, fraud, conspiracy are the matter; and the name of the whole atrocious mass is—HEEP!" (779)

The "mass" of corrupted "matter" is "HEEP." Then, carrying his pun to pure metaphor, as Uriah tries to stop his read-

ing of the letter of indictment against him, Micawber strikes
Uriah and cries out, "Approach me again, you—you—you
HEEP of infamy!" (p. 819). The "matter" now has meaning:
this "mass" of "matter" is now a "HEEP of infamy." Then,
at the end of the scene, David tells Uriah what he has learned
—or perhaps had proved to him—by this example of evil in
action and being. "There never were greed and cunning in
the world yet," he tells Uriah, "that did not do too much, and
overreach themselves. It is as certain as death" (pp. 828-29).

The last time we see Uriah is in the model prison, when
David and Tommy Traddles visit that "Tower of Babel."
Along with Littimer, Uriah has been sentenced to be trans-
ported for life; and as these two await the execution of their
sentences they have become pious and penitent "model pri-
sioners." David concludes that in this "they were perfectly
consistent and unchanged . . . that the hypocritical knaves
were just the subjects to make that sort of profession in such
a place; that they knew its market-value . . . in the immediate
service it would do them when they were expatriated" (p.
930). From his experience with and observation of Heep,
David has learned what the nature of evil is. That it is substantial in this world David acknowledges. He will not run from
it, or pretend that it doesn't exist. He doesn't need to—thanks
to his understanding of it.

David achieves his comprehension of both Jane Murdstone
and Uriah Heep through close attention to their gestures,
proceeding through discoverable stages from description to
metaphor to symbol and metaphysical identification. Comprehension, again, is the work of the imagination: it is the
primary responsibility of David the artist, his chief work in
life. And the way he goes about comprehending various characters, then, is an example of both the way Dickens works,
creating characters, and the way he proposes that we meet the
world. Because David is the narrator of this novel, these two
become one: David creates "characters" in his novel, and in
his life he meets and comprehends the world through those
characters. What this says is that, for Dickens, the artist is—
or should be—everyman. Only through the use of the comprehending imagination, he says, can everyman become free,
and wise.

NOTES

1. The final chapters of the novel name three daughters for David and Agnes: Agnes, then Dora, and then Betsey Trotwood, their "least child" (p. 947). There is no mention of a Clara—or, for that matter, of a new David; their "boys" are mentioned twice (pp. 939, 947), but without names.

2. Dickens's use of "peculiarities and oddities" to see the *worse* part of man is also remarkably accurate. Nancy Metz has collected more than fifty entries in medical literature crediting Dickens with discovering the symptomatic evidence for various diseases.

3. Presumably the complaint Dickens was answering was that contained in the review in *Fraser's Magazine*. See George Ford, *Dickens and His Readers*, pp. 13, 270, for reference to this review.

4. Manuscript bound with manuscript of *Oliver Twist*, Vol. 2B. Forster Collection, Victoria and Albert Museum, London.

5. "Metaphysical" is not a word foreign to Dickens, by the way. Harriet Carker speaks of the change in her brother John's character as "a metaphysical sort of change" in *Dombey and Son*, and Pip tells us that his first confusion at Miss Havisham's was "a case of metaphysics."

6. For a fuller representation of this, see my *Noah's Arkitecture: A Study of Dickens's Mythology*, pp. 70–71.

7. John Butt and Kathleen Tillotson, *Dickens at Work*, pp. 128–29.

8. The word in the manuscript is originally "garnished," which has connotations of fortification and defense and thus of arms and armaments—which is perhaps more appropriate to David's vision of her "dressed" than "embellished" is. "Embellished"—"made beautiful"—is more suited to her view of herself, and thus is an ironic usage in David's narrative.

9. The next reference to Miss Murdstone's metal gesture—later in the same chapter—was added by Dickens in the proofs for the novel. In the manuscript she is "smoothing her dress" as she speaks to her brother; in the revision he substitutes for this her "arranging the little fetters on her wrists" (Ms. 102/p. 172).

10. In trying to describe her nails Dickens writes "cold" and strikes it out twice before he finally says yes, her nails are indeed cold as steel, and writes the word in a third time to stay.

11. Steven Marcus has written at length about Daniel Quilp's sexuality, but to my knowledge no one has remarked on Uriah's sexuality, except to identify him—by his clammy hands—as a masturbator. (His writhing is sometimes accompanied by his hugging himself—like Fagin—which is also suggestive of masturbation.) It could be argued, I think, that Uriah's importance in the novel is largely sexual. When he is introduced he is described as something like an erect penis, though the small boy David doesn't recognize it as such. And David can't recognize Agnes's sexual identity either: to him she is a stained glass window, a sister, a saint. To Uriah, however, she is "the divinest of her sex," whom he "adores" and desires—hideously—to marry. It may be that what makes Uriah so hideous to David—and through his point of view, then, hideous to us—is his sexuality.

CHAPTER 4

"Who was never executed at the old Bailey."

In working with the full title of *David Copperfield* I have always paid the most attention to the three manuscript slips recording the title as "Mag's Diversions," because of the irony of the writer-as-magpie. I have also noted seriously—and been fascinated by—the sense of wholeness Dickens seems to be presuming for the book in the three slips devoted to "Copperfield Complete" and "Copperfield's Entire," and the four which call the book "The Copperfield Survey of the World as it Rolled." I have always been puzzled, however, by the four slips which do variations on "The Last Will and Testament of David Copperfield," made even more puzzling by the repeated notation that this particular David "was never executed at the old Bailey."

I have argued elsewhere[1] a relation between *Pickwick Papers* and *Oliver Twist,* to be found in Mr. Pickwick's retreat to Dulwich and Oliver's retirement to that quiet little village where all the good people of the novel go. Both retreats are retreats into death. Mr. Pickwick's is a natural death, really, since he is an old man and is now "determined on retiring" (p. 892) and in "the decline of life" (p. 893); but Oliver's is an unnatural one, since he is too young—at age eleven—to be retired from life yet. I suggested at the conclusion of this earlier argument that the full title of *Pickwick Papers—The Post-humous Papers of the Pickwick Club—* might well be adapted to fit *Oliver Twist:* that just as we get a strong sense of everything being posthumous when we get to the end of Mr. Pickwick's novel, so too do we get the sense at the end of Oliver's. The narrator assured us in the first paragraph of the novel that had the "item of mortality" we call Oliver Twist not survived his birth, "it is somewhat more than probable that these memoirs never would have appeared, or, if they had, being comprised within a couple of pages, that they would have [been] . . . the most concise and faithful specimen of biography extant in the literature" (p. 45). When we get to the final chapter of "these memoirs," it is only natural that we should remember this ironic note, and expect Oliver's end to coincide with the end of the novel—even though he is only eleven years old!

The metaphoric death of Oliver Twist, the boy who loves cemeteries, seems to me unsatisfactory as a solution or resolution to anything. The end of the novel leaves me more dissatisfied, more frustrated, than perhaps anything else I have ever read. Several years ago, on a visit to Oakham School in England, I was pleased to find some young children who shared my frustration. Talking about the novel with a group of twelve-year-olds, I began by eliciting their sympathy for Oliver, "cuffed and buffeted" and starved in the Workhouse. We then talked about his escape to London, his encounter with the Artful Dodger, and the results of this happy meeting. Everything in their response to the Artful was favorable—they overlooked the dirt and the ugliness—and Fagin stood out for them more as the man who fed Oliver and took care of the boys than as a criminal. They accepted Mr. Brownlow when he came along, in an unenthusiastic but polite way: "He's like what daddies are all supposed to be," one child said; and when I asked what the "supposed to be" meant, he said, "Oh, you know, sir, they're supposed to be perfect and able to do anything—but they never are." As we approached the end of the novel we began to talk about Oliver's at last finding happiness: the discovery of his identity, the recovery of his fortune, his adoption by Mr. Brownlow, and his friendship with his aunt Rose. We were all settling ourselves comfortably among these recollections of the novel's close when one boy suddenly registered a disturbed look and shook his head. As we went on he became more agitated, and finally started flagging his hand in the air. Before I could call on him—another child was speaking—he was on his feet, and blurted out in an earnest and anguished voice, "Please, sir! Mr. Brownlow has adopted Oliver and taken him away—but oh, sir! Mr. Fagin is dead, and there's nobody to take care of all those *other* little boys!" The effect of this insight was electric. Suddenly all the children were in excited sympathetic agreement with the first child in his concern for "all the *other* little boys"—and as frustrated by Dickens's conclusion as I was. Selective rescue from the world is unsatisfactory—from the world's point of view: and those children at Oakham School knew as well as I do that we are all in this world.

It seems to me that the passion of Dickens's career from *Oliver Twist* onward has been to find a way to let his characters stay in the world at the end of a novel. *The Old Curiosity Shop* —another novel about death as an escape—is a regression, thematically, rather than a forward step, but otherwise he works ahead regularly toward creating central characters strong enough and wise enough to survive in the large world. His ambition is for them to be able to begin the work of changing—of reforming or re-forming—this "mad world" through their strength and wisdom. David first manages to achieve this success for Dickens, in a very special way; and then Esther and Allan, Arthur Clennam and Little Dorrit, Pip, and finally Eugene and Lizzy, John and Bella, and Mortimer follow David's lead. Along the way, in the sermon called *Hard Times,* Dickens warns us sternly what will happen if we fail in our similar task; and in *A Tale of Two Cities* he creates a mythic future in which this mad world is indeed reformed, thanks to the final strength and wisdom—"Love," for Dickens, is "the highest wisdom" (ED, p. 130)—of Sidney Carton.

With the exception of Sidney, all of the heroes and heroines of these later novels are young people whom we can expect to use their wisdom in the world: to "turn to in earnest," as Eugene says (OMF, p. 885). They have all been "tried by adversity" (OT, p. 479), and have learned to love; and love is for Dickens what will enable them to live in this world. The living is what's important: that's what the love is for. "Everything that happens," he says, "shows beyond mistake that you can't shut out the world; that you are in it, to be of it; that you get yourself into a false position the moment you try to sever yourself from it; and that you must mingle with it, and make the best of it, and make the best of yourself into the bargain."[2]

But if the idea is to mingle with the world—to learn how to survive in it—then why does Dickens *begin* his thinking about *David Copperfield* with David's death? Why does he consider entitling it "The last living speech and confession of/David Copperfield the Younger/of Blunderstone House/Who was never executed at the old Bailey/Being his personal history, adventures, and worldy experiences?" Or "The last living speech and confession of/David Copperfield Junior/of Blunderstone Lodge/Who was never executed at the old Bailey/Being his personal history/Found among his papers"? Or "The Last Will and Testament/ of/Mr. David Copperfield/Being his personal history/Bequeathed as a legacy"; "The Copperfield Confessions/Being the personal history, experience, and observations of/Mr. David Copperfield/ of Blunderstone Lodge/Who was never executed at the old Bailey/Being his personal history." Why does Dickens presume, even before he begins this novel, that his hero is dead?

Several years ago I posed that question to a class which had been studying *David Copperfield,* and one very good student answered, "Because he *is* dead." Steve Thiry wasn't a student who disliked David; he wasn't being nasty. For him David was gloriously dead. Steve didn't know how or why this was so, but the language—the feeling, the sense—of "A Last Retrospect" told him such as he read it, and gave him a strange sense of peace.

I have long wondered at myself as I read *David Copperfield* each year, why as I approach the end of the novel I begin to read more and more slowly, dreading to finish it. It is not just that I don't want the story to end, though that certainly is part of it, however much I may disparage plot. Still, why shouldn't I want it to end? The end is what we call a happy one, after all, a full and rich one. Miss Betsey, Peggotty, and Mr. Dick are turned into something like immortals, Tommy Traddles is being touted for a judgeship, David and Agnes have happy children and are happy in each other. What's wrong?

Nothing is wrong, of course; everything is right. Yet Dickens felt the same way I do as he approached the end of the novel in writing it:

"I am within three pages of the shore; and I am strangely
divided, as usual in such cases, between sorrow and joy. . . . if I
were to say half of what *Copperfield* makes me feel tonight, how
strangely . . . I should be turned inside-out! I seem to be sending
some part of myself into the Shadowy World."[3]

"Three pages from the shore" means starting the final chapter, "A Last Retrospect"; and the "Shadowy World"—repeated without the capitals in the first Preface to the novel—
is where "the shadows which I now dismiss" (p. 950) must go
at the end. The Shadowy World is death's world: and David's
"shadows"—all the people he knows and has known, the
whole world of his novel and his life—must go there. The
world of his "personal history, adventures, experience, and
observation" dies as he completes it, removes himself from it,
and prepares to "travel on" (p. 946). Similarly, he thinks,
"realities [will melt] from me" "when I close my life indeed"
(p. 950).

The very serenity of this conclusion is what disturbs. The
presumption it entails is more than I can manage or accept at
first. As a reader, at the end of the novel I must give up either
David or his world—or so it seems. I must let go of one or the
other, though both by now have become "part of myself," and
like Dickens I don't want to send either of them "into the
Shadowy World." Once I have read through the end, however, and have closed the book, I find to my amazement that
I still have them both; and I call them now, together, *David
Copperfield.* And I see, suddenly, that David is indeed "the
hero of [his] own life" (p. 49).

Steve Thiry wasn't wrong in saying that, at the end, David
is dead. He is so in that he can release himself from this life,
separate himself from this world. In David, Dickens has
created a character who so fully accomplishes what he wanted
to accomplish that there is nothing to keep him in this life any
longer. David set out to recollect his life and thereby to learn
himself; his end, he said, was to find out "Whether I shall be
the hero of my own life" (p. 49). Having completed now his
self-analysis, and having comprehended his world, he can
leave that whole world behind him.

David's world, being whole, is also a representative world, and his comprehension of it is the thematic focus of the novel. At the end, David has grown wise, for Dickens; and there is nothing left for him to do but die. "I look back once more," he says as he begins the final chapter, "before I close these leaves" (p. 946); in the last paragraph he speaks of the time "when I close my life indeed" (p. 950)—and the pun in "close my life" is a useful one, for us and for Dickens. For Dickens, David's active comprehension of the wholeness or unity of the world and his own life—"these leaves" which we can now call "Copperfield Complete," perhaps—is what enables him to anticipate death so serenely. In this last chapter he has completed his "life"; and when he reaches the "close of [his] life indeed," he will expect that life to be whole and complete as well. Wisdom enables such serenity: and in order to be happy, we too must become wise.

Wordsworth's great ode is called "Intimations of Immortality"; but at the end the poet has learned how to accept *mortality,* and the last image—of "Thoughts that do often lie too deep for tears"—blows right "through death." It is the understanding, comprehending imagination—"the philosophic mind," he calls it—that takes Wordsworth there, transforming his earlier depression into a peaceful, joyful serenity which changes the meaning of death. For Wordsworth, now, death doesn't mean the "severing of our loves," any more than does Keats's ambition "to an[n]ihilate self."[4] At the end of Keats's "Hyperion: A Fragment," Apollo "become[s] immortal" through his achievement of a comprehension of life. "Knowledge enormous makes a God of me," he cries; and "Knowledge," as Douglas Bush says, means "not intellectual attainment, but a sympathetic understanding of the human condition which Keats . . . looked forward to as his highest aim."[5] Apollo rises to this state of immortal wisdom through mortality, "like . . . one who should take leave/Of pale immortal death, and . . . /Die into life." The achievement is tragic, and Keats breaks off the poem—there is nothing more to say.

In the retirement of Mr. Pickwick and the final retreat of Oliver Twist we sense that they are dying to the world, and that the world as it is goes on. At the end of *David Copperfield,* however, David *achieves* death, and within the mythic context of the novel we reach something very much like the end of the world—literally. While the novel is going on—while we are reading it—it is David's autobiography, not a novel. In "A Last Retrospect" David recalls everyone and everything one more time, not for us—so that we will know what has happened or will happen to the various characters—but for himself. He completes the world, thus, with his comprehension of it; and because complete things must cease to be in this real world of incompletion and change, all of *David Copperfield*— including David himself—is translated out of existence as soon as it ends. David puts down his pen—looking "upward," toward heaven—and everything dissolves into the "shadowy world" of the dead. What is left—*all* that is left!—for Dickens and for us is a memory, a recollection, a meaning, a book: the "legacy" of David Copperfield.

The effect of this conclusion is different, certainly, from that which we feel at the end of other novels, by Dickens or anybody else. I want to say that the effect is that of tragedy, except that "catharsis" is hardly what we feel. This tragedy is not Aristotle's; we are not "purged" or "cleansed" in any way, nor is the world. Indeed, the novel includes in its finale all those "unpurged elements"—the phrase is Yeats's—like Julia Mills and Jack Maldon; and just two chapters back we have seen Heep and Littimer, hardly eliminated from the world by imprisonment or transportation or any higher form of justice.

We are moved tremendously at the end of this novel: but the effect is the opposite of the relief and release of catharsis. The more appropriate term would seem to be kenosis, taken in a secular rather than theological sense. Catharsis signifies the purging of guilt, an often apocalyptic cleansing or purification as a result of which only the good remains. Kenosis, on the other hand, means simply an emptying out, a voiding or unburdening; in its theological sense it has to do with the Christian doctrine of Christ's "emptying himself" of his divinity in order to suffer and die as a man for men's redemption. At Christ's death, for the Christian, the best man becomes God again; however, he becomes God again not simply by reassuming his divine nature, but rather through the act of dying for us. "Greater love than this no man has, that he lay down his life for his friends": it is in this act of redeeming love that Christ both achieves his divinity again and sets an example for his followers. The focus which catharsis proposes is a negative one, on the elimination of evil; kenosis, on the other hand, focuses our attention positively, on the charitable act and its effect. If Aristotle were right about tragedy—or even about *Oedipus Rex*—we would leave the theatre relieved that the play is over and Oedipus banished from our midst. But we leave *Oedipus Rex* in awe at the nobility and heroic charity of Oedipus. At the end of the play, he is more a king for us than he has ever been before! And though we are in awe of him, we admire him; his love for his city, his respect for truth, and his personal determination for justice make him a hero whose values we would imitate. His example moves us, attracts us to its wisdom, enough that we may even forget his crimes. At the end of *Oedipus Rex* the point is not that Oedipus has been punished, or even that he has nobly punished himself, but that he has again saved Thebes.

Those who would follow Christ, now that he is gone from the race of men, must learn to imitate his love; his is the love which will perfect humanity. Similarly, if we are citizens of Thebes—if this world is Thebes—then we must learn to imitate Oedipus, now that he is gone from our midst. In both cases, we must fill the void created by loss or departure. They gave themselves for us: now we must give ourselves—for us.

As we finish *David Copperfield,* much the same kind of experience befalls us. We are attracted—naturally—to fill the void left by his fading into the shadowy realm of death or memory or fiction. We are so attracted because David has been wise: because he has been able to comprehend the world, and in so doing to create himself as "the hero of [his] life." And David's heroism is more important, I think, than that of any other hero—even that of Oedipus, or Lear, or Faust.[6]

David's heroism is important because the final emphasis is so strongly focused on what he learns, on his positive sense of the wholeness of his life. Yeats writes, in "Lapis Lazuli," of "Heaven blazing into the head" as "Tragedy wrought to its uttermost"; and "Heaven" in the "head" is the vision which he sees as the fit reward for characters like Lear.[7] We know this achievement in Lear or Oedipus, only momentarily and indirectly. We feel it as the final curtain falls, in that great welling up of emotion—of *sense*—which has come to us, and now leaves us exhausted and happy. In *David Copperfield* our experience is much the same. But David's achievement of that wisdom which we call tragic is not sudden or momentary, though it is still indirect. Wisdom is what he has been creating *as himself* since that evening in Switzerland when "great Nature spoke to [him]" (p. 887). And in the end, as we sense that David is about to pass away from among us, we are energized —serenely, deeply—to imitate him, to try to become his wisdom. His "death" will leave a vacuum in the valley of life which we will feel drawn to fill, with love. David has made his world our world, and in so doing has taught us to love it.

David's death, then, is not escape, like Mr. Pickwick's or Oliver's. Rather, David dies in answer to their deaths, for Dickens: David dies in and for the world, triumphantly, tragically, wisely, lovingly. His death is more like Sidney Carton's, except that Sidney's death is admittedly the narrator's dream —"If he had given utterance to his [thoughts], and they were prophetic, they would have been these" (p. 404)—in an historical fiction, and thus quite unreal; whereas David's death comes at or as the end of an autobiography. As an autobiography, however, *David Copperfield* ends not just with its final paragraph, but with the preface which Dickens wrote immediately after the last paragraph. In the preface he admits that "this Book" is but the end result of "a two years' imaginative task" dealing with "the creatures of his brain"; and he then confesses—insists—"that no one can ever believe this Narrative, in the reading, more than I have believed it in the writing." The truth which "this Narrative" creates and teaches— and which Dickens believes—enables him "instead of looking backward" to "look forward." It is the first of his novels to do so; and though his "mind is . . . divided between pleasure and regret," he casts "a hopeful glance" toward the future—because *David Copperfield* and what it means have "made [him] happy" (p. 45).

Dickens is always a serious novelist, even as a very young

man. He is seeking wisdom and happiness in this world from
the beginning. Mr. Pickwick is a comic parody of a philosopher, and one of the hints at the seriousness underneath the
comedy of *Pickwick Papers* is the use of the word "philosopher" in relation to its hero. The limits of Mr. Pickwick's
knowledge and experience of the world are described in the
title of the brilliant paper he has just read to the Pickwick Club
in the opening chapter: "Speculations on the Source of the
Hampstead Ponds, with some Observations on the Theory of
Tittlebats" (p. 67). Beyond this, all he has is his innocence
and his benevolence. The first of these is abused by the world,
and all but destroyed; the second seems somehow to be available to Mr. Pickwick as a virtue only when he is drunk. Mr.
Pickwick is lovely, loving, generous, gentle, and kind—but he
is hardly wise, though he is sometimes called a "philosopher."
Mr. Blotton is more than right when, in the opening chapter,
he calls Mr. Pickwick a "humbug" (p. 71). There is more
wrong with this world than Mr. Pickwick comprehends.

When Oliver Twist first enters Mr. Brownlow's study, after
recovering from his fever, he is reported to us as "marvelling
where the people could be found to read such a great number
of books as seemed to be written to make the world wiser" (p.
144). Mr. Brownlow proposes to him that someday he may
read them, and tells him not to judge significance by size:
some large books are "heavy," but "there are other equally
heavy ones, though of a much smaller size." Then, curiously,
Mr. Brownlow asks Oliver, "How should you like to grow up
a clever man, and write books, eh?" (p. 145). Oliver doesn't,
of course: he couldn't write books even if he wanted to, because Dickens doesn't let him "grow up," or "grow up" in the
world. And the only place wisdom can be found, for Dickens,
is in this world: in this world, and of it—to "make the best of
it."

But then it must be true, it would seem, that if David dies
at the end of his novel—and goes *out* of this world—either he
has failed to attain wisdom, or having attained it loses it in his
death. Neither of these formulations is accurate, however, or
acceptable. David does become wise in his novel, and he does
in effect die. But he dies as a result of his wisdom—and this

Dickens seems to have planned or known or expected from his first days of title-planning. David dies, and what he leaves us as his "legacy," as his "Last Will and Testament"—which we call *David Copperfield*—is that wisdom.

Wisdom is not something that you acquire; rather, it is something that you give away. Like happiness, or pleasure, it won't stay within: much like God's grandeur, for Hopkins, it "gathers to a greatness"—and it "will flame out, like shining from shook foil."[8] Wisdom is a social virtue: it radiates, naturally.

The philosopher's stone was once the goal of all of man's explorations. What it promised—if found—was wisdom. Somewhere along the way toward the modern world, however, values began to change, and greed short-circuited the search for that light. By Chaucer's time, the alchemist had ceased to have wisdom or even the universal panacea as his end; instead, he pursued the knowledge that would transmute baser metals into gold. Once gold had been a symbol for wisdom, representing the untarnishing ideal of human and earthly perfection. But we somehow became distracted by that shiny symbol, and it became an end in itself. Wisdom was unseated, the spiritual value replaced by something of physical worth. Symbolically, the scarcity of gold suggests only the difficulty of attaining wisdom; but when gold ceases to be a symbol and becomes itself the object of our pursuit, its meaning changes, and our attitude toward it changes. Whereas all men could pursue wisdom, without any danger of its running out even if everyone grew wise, we must compete for gold— or forge it, out of baser stuff. To become wise, we must transform only ourselves; but to get enough gold we would transform that which is not us into gold, and hoard it to ourselves.

For Dickens, hoarding gold is corrupt and corrupting. In *David Copperfield* such meanness gives comic pain to Barkis, and is the source of Uriah Heep's downfall. By the time of *Our Mutual Friend,* fourteen years later, hoarded gold—Harmon's gold—is not in fact gold at all, but simply money: it rusts and tarnishes like baser metals do (OMF, pp. 429, 849). At its best, for Dickens, gold reflects the light of good people's wise use of it; but wisdom, he says, is itself a source of light. It radiates, and has a "power of doing good" (p. 915). It gives itself away, naturally. And when we're really wise, truly and fully wise, we give everything away.

Ralph Ellison's hero asks himself, in the epilogue to *Invisible Man,* "So why do I write, torturing myself to put it down?" And he answers: "Because in spite of myself I've learned some things." And learning—it's wisdom that he is talking about—won't stay inside. The Invisible Man "couldn't be still in hibernation. Because, damn it, there's the mind, the *mind.* It wouldn't let me rest."[9] Like David, the Invisible Man has to recollect his life, in order to understand himself and this world. The act of recollective understanding—Ellison calls it "hibernation"—is not an end in itself, as Ellison insists in the prologue to the novel: "Please, a definition: A hibernation is a covert preparation for a more overt action."[10]

In its sublime role as the creator of understanding, the mind is a metaphor for God, and acts as we say God acts, loving what he creates by creating it. The mind doesn't need any other justification for its activity. It knows that being—or loved being—is useful in itself, and that "everything" then can "give [it] pleasure" (CB, I, p. 131).

The mind is essentially erotic. It requires sensory stimulation for its pleasure. The body tries to satisfy it, gives it as much stimulation as it can; but that is never enough—so the mind creates more stimulation for itself, by imagining. The imagination remembers the past and dreams alternate presents and futures in order to satisfy the mind.

Being essentially erotic, the mind is also essentially charitable—as anything erotic should be. And what the mind does, when it creates pleasure for itself through the imagination, is give that pleasure to the senses. Of course, part of the reason the mind shares its pleasures with the senses is to get them back—as sensory experience. The body sends what it feels always back to the mind, by nerve express.

The important point to be made is that the mind doesn't differentiate between what comes in from the senses, as experience, and what goes out through them, as expression. Experience and expression are simultaneous—or simply one—in the mind. What comes in as experience becomes pleasure, or meaning; and when the mind grows happy and wise with sensory or imaginative experience, it generates—articulates, communicates, radiates—substantial happiness and wisdom in the world as its expression. It creates itself outside itself, and begins to change this world.

Dickens always believes that goodness, joy, happiness, and wisdom radiate. Mr. Pickwick "beams" with benevolence throughout the earlier part of his novel; Oliver's goodness shines in his face for everyone from Brownlow to Nancy to Toby Crackit—who says, prophetically, "His mug is a fortun' to him" (p. 209). This kind of radiance is typical of the early novels, through *Dombey and Son.* Like his benevolence, Mr. Pickwick's radiance is not very effective or useful in the world; and Oliver's radiance, though it moves Nancy and attracts Brownlow's attention, saves only Oliver. In the later novels, however, virtues like goodness, joy, happiness, and wisdom radiate usefully and importantly, and radiance begins both to define individual characters and to underline social themes.

Radiance becomes a principle for Esther Summerson, as she sets out "to do some good to some one, and win some love" (p. 64) and proposes "to be as useful as I could, and to render what kind services I could, to those immediately around me; and to try to let that circle of duty gradually and naturally expand itself" (p. 164). She knows that radiance is indeed natural, and is "happy in the power of doing a great deal of good" (p. 668). When Allan asks her to marry him, it is because of the "many hearts she touches and awakens," and the "love she wins" (p. 889).

In *Hard Times,* Sissy radiates goodness which affects everyone from Mr. Gradgrind to Rachael to Loo and her sister Jane, whose "beaming face" is "Sissy's doing" (p.243). In *Little Dorrit,* Amy's "purity and goodness" are radiant; Clennam sees them once, for example, "in their brightest light" (p. 472). At the end of *A Tale of Two Cities*—before Dickens makes up what Sidney Carton would have said had he spoken —we are told that as he ascended to the guillotine his face "was the peacefullest man's face ever beheld there," and that "he looked sublime and prophetic" (p. 403). In *Great Expecta-*

tions it is Joe who is radiant, and his "influence . . . flies out into the world" (p. 135).[11]

Our Mutual Friend is so full of images of radiance that radiance becomes a major theme in the novel. There are seemingly casual mentions of the "golden bower" of Jenny's hair as "radiant" (p. 335) and of "cordial bottles" that are cordially "radiant with fictitious grapes" (p. 145). Even Podsnap presumes to be radiant, with a "light in [his] countenance" which has "irradiated" society (p. 684)—for Podsnap, this is the "light" which society should see by—and Mrs. Wilfer has a special talent for "glaring" (p. 678). But the truly radiant people are Henrietta Boffin, John Rokesmith, and Bella. There is "always . . . radiance on Mrs. Boffin's face" (p. 363), and "the look of her radiant face" is "reviving" to Betty Higden (p. 443); Henrietta has a "radiant nature" (p. 387) and a "radiant face" (p. 842), and smiles "most radiantly" (p. 841). John Rokesmith has a "beaming face" and gives Bella a "radiant look" (p. 583) that both knows and loves her. There is "brightness" and "light" in Bella's face (p. 594), and when she and John are married she is "a bright light" in their home (p. 750). The whole world turns something like radiant for their wedding, thanks to their love and the "gracious sun" (p. 739); and even Pa Wilfer—who significantly has "no egotism in his pleasant nature"—is "radiant" (p. 753) after their marriage.

Mr. Crisparkle's name is the closest the language of *The Mystery of Edwin Drood* comes to radiance. There is a glow, to be sure, from the opium pipe at the Princess Puffer's, and John Jasper suffers from a fire that burns inside him; but this short last novel is generally too dark for radiant imagery. The real radiance of *Edwin Drood* is the light in Dickens's eye—but that argument must wait until later.

The point I want to make now is that Dickens's regular use of radiance as a gesture, then a principle, and finally the symbol for a theme or a theme itself, is indicative of his belief in human goodness and the possibility of human wisdom, and his determination to find a way for goodness and wisdom to influence this world for the better. He finds the way, of course: finds it first in *David Copperfield,* in the "growing reputation" which comes from David's "Story . . . of my experience" (p. 889), in his "growing reputation and success" which "enlarge [his] power of doing good" (p. 915). From trying "to get a better understanding of myself and be a better man" (p. 890), David begins, for Dickens, to make this world a better world. Mr. Chillup is worried about David's using his mind so much as he must, in his work—"There must be great excitement. . . . You must find it a trying occupation" (p. 904); "And this action of the brain now, sir? Don't you find it fatigue you?" (p. 905)—but Mr. Micawber knows that David's is the "Eagle course," and that its value is that we may "watch it, with delight, with entertainment, with instruction" (p. 945).

For Dickens, *David Copperfield* is very much one of those books "written to make the world wiser." The wisdom it proposes to us is the wisdom of the imagination. Mr. Pickwick has no imagination to speak of, and Mr. Brownlow doesn't trust or respect it.[12] But David is always an imaginative creature; and what he achieves through the agency of his imagination is the comprehension of the world to which, in the end, he gives his name.

We cherish *David Copperfield* in part, perhaps, because it is a life, a whole life. In this world of fragments and incompletions, one of the things art does for us is create wholes: and *David Copperfield* is significantly whole. As Dickens works through his trial titles he creates for himself the idea of this novel as about a "whole" or "complete" or "entire" life or world; and then he carries that idea through to its logical conclusion, and creates a novel that is a memoir, left to us by its author, "found among his papers."

Of course, there is a long tradition of "found" manuscripts in the history of fiction, and Dickens has used the device himself in *Pickwick Papers* and in the scheme of *Master Humphrey's Clock*. But in neither of those undertakings nor elsewhere in the works of other, earlier novelists is there anything quite like *David Copperfield* as a first person narrative.[13] The last line of Dickens's title—"Which he never meant to be published on any account"—and the first sentence of David's narrative assure us of this. "These pages" are in a very special sense David's life.

That David "was never executed at the old Bailey" says simply that David dies a natural death. His "legacy" is the wisdom which has taught him that death *is* natural, as happiness should be. And the happiness which I feel then, at the end of this novel—for all of my dread of finishing it—tells me that David hasn't died at all, finally: rather, he has given me his life!

NOTES

1. In *Noah's Arkitecture: A Study of Dickens's Mythology* (Ohio University Press, 1972), pp. 13–20.
2. Dickens to Wilkie Collins, 6 September 1858.
3. John Forster, *The Life of Charles Dickens* (Everyman edition), volume 2, p. 98.
4. Wordsworth, "Ode: Intimations of Immortality," lines 206–07, 189–90, 192. Keats to Benjamin Bailey, 10 June 1818.
5. *Hyperion: A Fragment,* book 3, line 113. Bush's note appears in *Selected Poems and Letters of John Keats* (Riverside edition), p. 338.
6. If David has a parallel in our culture's history, it is Dante. But that comparison will have to wait.
7. "Lapis Lazuli," lines 16–20.
8. "God's Grandeur," lines 2–3.
9. *Invisible Man* (Vintage edition), pp. 437, 433.
10. *Invisible Man,* p. 11.
11. Joe's own articulation of the principle of radiance is rather cryptic, as his attempts at serious speech always are: being "friends," Joe calculates, will "lead to larks" (GE, p. 128).
12. When Mr. Brownlow is first attracted to "something in [Oliver's] face," he dismisses the intimation of familiarity saying, "No . . . it must be imagination" (p. 119). Later, when Nancy has premonitions of her death he dismisses them in the same way, as "Imagination" (p. 409).
13. *Moby Dick* (1851) is probably the closest to *David Copperfield* among works of fiction, provided we keep our attention on Ishmael. There are also remarkable similarities between this novel and Dante's *Divine Comedy,* as I mentioned earlier, and between this novel and Wordsworth's *Prelude* (1850).

CHAPTER 5

"Which he never meant to be published on any account."

Peggotty tells the child David of his mother's death. Then the narrator writes:

> From the moment of my knowing of the death of my mother, the idea of her as she had been of late had vanished from me. I remembered her, from that instant, only as the young mother of my earliest impressions. . . . What Peggotty had told me now, was so far from bringing me back to the later period, that it rooted the earlier image in my mind. It may be curious, but it is true. In her death she winged her way back to her calm untroubled youth, and cancelled all the rest.
>
> The mother who lay in the grave, was the mother of my infancy; the little creature in her arms, was myself, as I had once been, hushed forever in her bosom. (186–87)

Burying himself with his mother—replacing her other baby with himself—is the unwanted orphan child's way back to security and happiness. "Hushed" on his mother's breast, he is symbolically—fantastically—solaced by her love. Rather than bury his happy childhood—by "burying his past," as we would say—David buries himself as a child in order to keep that past. Under the stress of his mother's death, the boy performs an act of memory so strong that it takes him and his mother back to the time of his infancy: back to the first chapter, to "I am Born." And *David Copperfield* begins again.

In a sense the "personal History . . . of David Copperfield" is now over; the next phase is that of the "Adventures . . . of David Copperfield" in the world. But the adventuring David is a new David. He recreates himself now, separate from both the old life and the old self. "I begin Life on my own Account" (p. 208) is the new chapter-title version of "I am Born."[1] David finds and makes his way in the world, now, on his own.

He determines to run away from London, and seek refuge with Betsey Trotwood; and though his aunt accepts him and takes him in, she also immediately turns him out again, sending him off to Dr. Strong's school in Canterbury to "make another beginning" (p. 272). And her reason for this, as she tells Mr. Wickfield, is "to make the child happy and useful" (p. 277). That phrase—"happy and useful"—will echo throughout the novel, from this point on. David's remembering it—recording it—so frequently tells us of its significance for him even before we find out what it actually means; for the present, we need only note what kind of plan Miss Betsey has for David in proposing that he learn to be "happy and useful." She expects him to live in the world, obviously: and she expects him to manage and order his life there according to qualities, virtues, and principles. What she wants David "to do" in deciding on a career for himself is very different, for example, from what Mr. Brownlow has in mind as a career for Oliver when he first takes him in. When Oliver's savior talks with him about his future, he first proposes, teasingly, that the boy might wish to grow up and "write books," but then promises "not to make an author of [him], while there's an honest trade to be learnt, or brickmaking to turn to" (p. 145). Oliver marvels all on his own at the shelves of books "written to make the world wiser" (p. 144); Mr. Brownlow, however, thinks of a trade as occupation for the child—and that kind of being "useful" is more like picking oakum than it is like what Miss Betsey has in mind for David's future, which he must earn, and learn.

The character David continues his new life straight through his adolescence, looking always toward the future. The first return he makes to his Blunderstone past—to his life before his mother's death and his burial of that life with her—comes after he leaves school, when Miss Betsey sends him off to visit Peggotty at Yarmouth. His aunt wants him to determine "what [he] would like to be" (p. 330); and to help him "to know [his] own mind" (p. 331) on this metaphysical as well as professional question, she sends him back to his past. Then, while he is visiting Peggotty—who has been absent from the

novel since just after his mother's death—he goes back, for
the first time, to Blunderstone:

> my occupation in my solitary pilgrimages was to recall every yard
> of the old road as I went along it, and to haunt the old spots, of
> which I never tired. I haunted them, as my memory had often
> done, and lingered among them as my younger thoughts had
> lingered when I was far away. The grave beneath the tree, where
> both my parents lay—on which I had looked out, when it was my
> father's only, with such curious feelings of compassion, and by
> which I had stood, so desolate, when it was opened to receive my
> pretty mother and her baby—the grave which Peggotty's own
> faithful care had ever since kept neat, and made a garden of, I
> walked near, by the hour. . . . My reflections at these times were
> always associated with the figure I was to make in life, and the
> distinguished things I was to do. My echoing footsteps went to
> no other tune, but were as constant to that as if I had come to
> build my castles in the air at a living mother's side. (378)

But David has no "living mother" to come home to, or even
a "home" at Blunderstone. The details which David the character's imagination creates to impress these facts on his consciousness are deep ones:

> There were great changes in my old home. The ragged nests,
> so long deserted by the rooks, were gone; and the trees were
> lopped and topped out of their remembered shapes. The garden
> had run wild, and half of the windows of the house were shut up.
> It was occupied, but only by a poor lunatic gentleman, and the
> people who took care of him. He was always sitting at my little
> window, looking out into the churchyard. . . .
> Our old neighbours, Mr. and Mrs. Grayper, were gone to
> South America, and the rain had made its way through the roof
> of their empty house, and stained the outer walls. Mr. Chillup was
> married again to a tall, raw-boned, high-nosed wife; and they had
> a weazen little baby, with a heavy head that it couldn't hold up,
> and two weak staring eyes, with which it seemed to be always
> wondering why it had ever been born. (378–79)

With the nests gone—the trees radically altered from "their
remembered shape"—the rookery that wasn't a rookery may
never even have been. The "poor lunatic gentleman" in David's window is Dickens's proof that David can't indulge the
"fancies" he once enjoyed there—or, if he can, then proof for
Dickens that those fancies themselves are mad, are folly. The

past is past, and the function of memory is *not* to enable us to return there. The departure of the Graypers—a suggestive but not immediately disturbing fact—is modified into a violent representation of the destruction of David's Blunderstone past by the derelict state of their house. The house deserves this fate, in a sense, since it was from there that Clara Copperfield was married to Edward Murdstone, to begin all this destruction. Mr. Chillup's "weazen little baby"—born, I suppose, out of Dickens's pained and painful imagination— is another sign of the world of unhappy accident which has replaced the simple, idyllic world that Blunderstone once seemed to be, and to which David is trying to return.

What David sees in his visits to his childhood home—he goes, it seems, almost every day during his Yarmouth visit— is that the past is utterly gone. "But," he says, "when the place was left behind . . . it was delicious to think of having been there" (p. 379). At night, however, sitting in his room in the houseboat, he avoids Blunderstone in his reveries, and reflects only upon the present: "[I] remembered with a grateful heart how blest I was in having such a friend as Steerforth, such a friend as Peggotty, and such a substitute for what I had lost as my excellent and generous aunt" (p. 379).

Part of the reason for David's writing this book is to enable him to go back to Blunderstone, but in a different way. He must go back to reclaim that life for himself, to become— again—"David Copperfield of Blunderstone Rookery." He goes back there unknowingly, of course, in his courtship of Dora and in their life together. The repetition of Clara Copperfield in David's "child wife" has often been noted, as has the repetition of Murdstone's attempt at "forming" his mother's "character" (p. 100) in David's trying to "form" Dora's "mind" (p. 762). David catches himself imitating Murdstone, and recovers; then he and Dora find a way to be "happy" together for a year and more before she dies.

This "happiness" is not real happiness, however, and David admits it: "I was happy; but the happiness I had vaguely anticipated, once, was not the happiness I enjoyed, and there was always something wanting" (p. 765). And with this admission David the narrator calls attention to himself as narrator

again: "In fulfillment of that compact I have made with myself, to reflect my mind on this paper, I again examine [what
I felt], closely, and bring its secrets to the light" (p. 765). To
"reflect his mind on this paper," what the narrator must
recreate is how the character felt: not for the sake of the
feeling, but in order to know what the feeling meant. What he
finds in doing this is that David the character missed in Dora
"something that had been a dream of my youthful fancy; that
was incapable of realization; that I was now discovering to be
so, with some natural pain, as all men did" (p. 765).

The ambition that Dora does not fulfill is David's ambition
for fairyland. As a child, David thought that he and his mother
"had always lived . . . in the happiest state imaginable, and
lived so then"; and as far as David was concerned, they "always meant to live so" (pp. 84–85). When he first visits Mr.
Peggotty's houseboat, that small "ark" seems to him "a perfect abode" (p. 78), "the most delicious retreat that the imagination of man could conceive" (p. 82), with "the completest
and most desirable bedroom ever seen" (pp. 79–80) just for
him. He is not content with Emily's being "a most beautiful
little girl" (p. 80); with his "fancy" he makes "a very angel of
her" (p. 87).

David spends a lot of his youthful energy "building castles
in the air," and insisting on the superlative in everything.
When he first sees Dora he falls madly in love "in an instant."
But it is not really Dora he falls in love with: "She was more
than human to me. She was a Fairy, a Sylph . . . anything that
no one ever saw, and everything that everybody ever wanted"
(p. 450). When he is with Dora he is "wandering in a garden
of Eden all the while" (p. 452), a creature lost "in Fairyland"
(p. 456). When Dora fails David, she fails because reality
creeps into fairyland—as it always does, for all of us.

The partial happiness which David eventually creates for
himself and Dora is a stoical compromise with frustration
more than it is happiness, and David is haunted by his mistake
in marrying her—by their "unsuitability in mind and purpose" (p. 766)—for the rest of her life. When she dies, however, he is not freed; instead, her death unites in his mind with
all the other losses and disappointments he has suffered since

his mother's death, and weighs him down to near despair. He does not include his mother's death in his collection of losses now, because her death closed another life, separate from this, for him; he mourns now for the deaths of Dora, Steerforth, and Ham, and the displacement of Mr. Peggotty and "the wandering remnants of the simple home, where I had heard the night-wind blowing, when I was a child" (p. 886). His grief, he says, is for "all that I had lost—love, friendship, interest; [for] all that had been shattered—my first trust, my first affection, the whole airy castle of my life; [for] all that remained—a ruined blank and waste, lying wide around me, unbroken, to the dark horizon" (p. 886). What he laments is the failure of his youthful dream of happiness, his young ambition for a simple, happy life. "From the accumulated sadness into which I fell," he says, "I had at length no hope of ever issuing again. . . . I believed that I should die" (p. 886).

David begins to recover from this "despondency," this near-death, through the healing, teaching influence of Nature. His disappointment, the narrator David says, has left him empty: "I had no purpose, no sustaining soul within me, anywhere" (p. 887). Then, in the Alps, a change begins to take place, the emptiness to be filled. Isolated in his disappointed, empty self, he has been able to feel nothing but his own sorrow. His dreams all gone, he finds himself purposeless, soulless. As he begins to think of dying, he so empties himself that he loses self, and becomes selfless. Then "in those awful solitudes" of the mountains he feels first "sublimity and wonder," and after that "some long unwonted sense of beauty and tranquility" (p. 887). Finally, "all at once, in this serenity, great Nature spoke to me; and soothed me to lay down my weary head upon the grass, and weep as I had not wept yet, since Dora died!" (p. 887).

These tears are different from those David shed for "all that [he] had lost" earlier. The narrator commented then: "If my grief were selfish, I did not know it to be so" (p. 886). It *was* selfish, of course; and selfish sorrow obliterates the world with its tears. Now David's tears wash away the sorrow, cleanse his vision, and reunite him with the world. "I sought out Nature, never sought in vain," the narrator David tells us; "and I

admitted to my breast the human interest I had so lately
shrunk from" (p. 889). The "human interest" he feels now is
like what his younger self felt after the first desparate pain of
his mother's death was over. The sorrow he felt then, the
child David told Peggotty, "makes me feel kinder" (p. 188).[2]

Kind feelings turn out from the self to the world, and turn
the self out into the world, to live. Wordsworth writes in the
"Intimations Ode" of "soothing thoughts that spring/Out of
human suffering," and concludes triumphantly with the pro-
leptic assertion, drawn from his own experience,

> Thanks to the human heart by which we live,
> Thanks to its tenderness, its joys, and fears,
> To me the meanest flower that blows can give
> Thoughts that do often lie too deep for tears.

When David recovers from his almost mystical experience in
the valley in the Alps, he opens the packet of letters he had
planned to read when he set out, and reads a letter from
Agnes: "She knew (she said) how such a nature as mine would
turn affliction to good. She knew how trial and emotion would
exalt and strengthen it. She was sure that in my every purpose
I should gain a firmer and a higher tendency, through the
grief I had undergone" (p. 888). Then, "inspired" by Agnes,
he begins to write again. First he writes "a Story, with a
purpose growing, not remotely, out of my experience"; and
then he sets to work "on a new fancy, which took strong
possession of me. . . . my third work of fiction" (p. 889).

In the last stanza of the "Intimations Ode," that "meanest
flower that blows" is obviously not just any flower, but "the
pansy at my feet" which had earlier told Wordsworth "of
something that is gone," "the glory and the dream" of the
world as he once saw it, "apparelled in celestial light." What
he accomplishes in the poem is to recollect the world, and
from the perspective of "sober" and "philosophic"—imaginative—acceptance, transform his experience of it from innocent yet selfish pleasure into love. The lament of the opening
stanza—"There was a time when meadow, grove, and stream
. . ."—is answered in the beginning of the last stanza: "And
O, ye Fountains, Meadows, Hills, and Groves,/Forebode not
any severing of our loves!" Likewise, David must recollect

and accept his world, and learn through the act of recollection how to love it. This is what he begins to do, in earnest—and as an artist—in Switzerland. Early on in the book, David narrator remarks of his child-self, "I could observe in little pieces, as it were"—but anything else "was, as yet, beyond me" (p. 70). At the end, he can hold all the pieces of this world together, happily and meaningfully, in his imagination—and then can let them go.

For Dickens just as for Coleridge, the way the imagination creates meaning is metaphoric. It "dissolves, diffuses, dissipates, in order to re-create," for Coleridge; to find meaning and to create new knowledge, "it struggles to idealize and to unify."[3] "All knowledge," he says, "rests on the coincidence of an object with a subject," or "mind."[4] The idealization or unification which the imagination seeks is that highest kind of knowledge through which the mind both holds together all the parts of its world and relates itself to them.[5] It makes the individual pieces of life—events, characters, places—coincide metaphorically with each other and with the self which experiences them, creating out of this conjunction what we have called since Socrates' time a life of meaning. Then, through another metaphoric operation, that life is completed—raised to a higher level as life—in the relation of the reflective self or "mind" to the world of its experience. This completion of life is comprehension: the act of holding together joined with the act of knowing. In Dickens's terms—or David's—such comprehension is what is achieved by "the blending of experience and imagination" (p. 734): the details of experience, closely observed, are transformed by the power of the imagination, into "ideal" or "unified" life.

Dickens rarely speaks of anything being "ideal" or "unified"; those are not value words for him. For him—and for David—the ideal life is the happy life, and that word appears over and over as *David Copperfield* nears its end. But happiness has been important throughout the novel. The narrator David often focuses his attention on his happiness or unhappiness, weighing and evaluating his experiences in those particular terms. Miss Betsey hopes that the young David will grow up to be "happy and useful," and those words regularly appear together thereafter. Agnes is always "happy and useful"; can David become so? And what does it mean to be happy and useful? Is it heroic to be happy and useful?

To understand what happiness means in *David Copperfield*— and I think that it means everything, finally—we will have to understand the relations Dickens sees among happiness, memory, and imagination. To do this we will have to think of happiness both as a virtue—and thus its own reward—and as a state of being. We will have to free memory from its usual time-orientation, and conceive of it again as a function of the imagination. And we will have to recognize the imagination as substantial, as the spirit which literally forms and informs matter, and through such forming and informing creates meaning.

Let me turn to *A Christmas Carol* again, where these relationships are presented more simply. Scrooge's imagination takes him on a three-part journey through his past, the immediate future which becomes the present when he awakens, and the future that is yet before him unless he change his ways. The spirits who lead him on this journey may be the creatures of a dream and the result of indigestion—"an undigested bit of beef . . . a fragment of an underdone potato" (p. 59)—but Scrooge believes in them and in what they show him. He promises to "live in the Past, the Present, and the Future" in order to learn "the lessons that they teach" (p. 126) about the meaning of life. And looking at the world, then—knowing that what life means is not competition or getting ahead or self, but being "in the world, and of it"—Scrooge finds "that everything could yield him pleasure" (p. 131).

Happiness and meaning are both products of the imagination. And just as expression and experience are the same, undifferentiated phenomenon to the mind, so the imaginative achievement of happiness need not be distinguished from that of meaning. They are the same. For Dickens, what I know will make me happy.

But what does being "useful" mean? The answer is clear and straightforward, whether we look at David himself for our definition or at any number of other characters. I want to consider two kinds of useful people before considering David's usefulness. The first are those who have been hurt by or in the world, and rendered useless to themselves and to society, who then must learn to be useful. Among this group are Mr. Dick, Miss Betsey, and Mrs. Gummidge. The second are the innocent creatures who are always useful, who ignore their own hurts or misfortunes in serving others. The best examples of this set are Peggotty and Tommy Traddles.

Though Mr. Dick gives Miss Betsey useful advice—it saves David, certainly, when he arrives at Dover—the occasions when his advice is needed are too few to keep him busy; and his work on the Memorial, though purposeful, is hardly useful. The Memorial is rather the product of Mr. Dick's unhappiness, and the emblem of his frustration in this "mad world." When David goes on to Dr. Strong's school at Canterbury, Mr. Dick wants to do things for him, and wants to buy things for the other boys; but he is "only allowed to rattle his money, and not to spend it" (p. 307). When Miss Betsey is "ruined," financially, Mr. Dick begins "to fret and worry himself out of spirits and appetite, as having nothing useful to do," and David determines to find a way either of "caus[ing] him to believe that he was useful" or of making him "really useful" (p. 589). Mr. Dick's own ideas of usefulness in this crisis are not very practical: "There's the Memorial—"(p. 561); "You see . . . if I could exert myself, Mr. Traddles—if I could beat a drum—or blow anything!" (p. 590). Traddles finds work for him, as a legal copyist; and "from the moment of his being usefully employed," he is "happy," and has "postponed the Memorial to a more convenient time" (p. 591).

At the end of the novel, Mr. Dick finds a more appropriate employment than either "memorializing the Lord Chancellor, or the Lord Somebody or other" (p. 201)[6] or copying legal documents for silver sixpences. David the artist has relieved him of the need to write the Memorial, and Miss Betsey's fortune is restored; but Mr. Dick still needs—naturally—to be useful. The last we see of him he is "an old man making giant kites" for the entertainment of David's children, "and gazing at them in the air, with a delight for which there are no words" (p. 947).

Miss Betsey is the one who first pairs "happy and useful"

(p. 277) as a single ideal, in explaining her ambition for David to Mr. Wickfield. Her own usefulness is in part in her good advice to David, which she begins to give him as she turns him over to Dr. Strong for his schooling: "Never," she tells him, "be mean in anything; never be false; never be cruel" (p. 280). And urging him to be "always natural and rational" (p. 331) as he leaves school, she says:

> "But what I want you to be, Trot . . . I don't mean physically, but morally; you are very well physically—is, a firm fellow. A fine firm fellow, with a will of your own. With resolution. . . . With determination. With character, Trot—with strength of character that is not to be influenced, except on good reason, by anybody, or by anything." (332)

Finally, as she sets David forward into the world, hoping "to provide for [his] being a good, a sensible, and a happy man," she tells him, "It's in vain, Trot, to recall the past, unless it works some influence upon the present" (p. 407). Miss Betsey has not herself lived by this wise rule, and both her happiness and her usefulness have thus been limited. She enters the novel planning to be useful to David's sister; thwarted in this plan—it comes from "her own old wrongs . . . working within her" (p. 55)—she retires. She tries then to hide or deny her past, and spends her life defending that symbolic "patch of green" (p. 251) in front of her house from the stubbornly aggressive reality of donkeys. But her care for Mr. Dick and then David takes her beyond herself and "her own old wrongs"; eventually her care for David even takes her out into the large world again, and at the end of the novel she is immortalized as "a steady walker of six miles at a stretch in winter weather" (p. 947).

Mrs. Gummidge is a minor character, almost a caricature. She has but three things to do in the novel, three gestures which both create her and give her and her role meaning. First she is "a lone lorn creetur' . . . and everythink goes contrairy with [her]" (p. 88)—and the comic misspelling of "everythink" is serious, since Mrs. Gummidge makes all the contrairies in her mind, dwelling on the death of "the old un" (p. 90). When Emily runs away, Mrs. Gummidge changes— "what have *my* contraries ever been to this," she says to Mr.

Peggotty (pp. 515–16)—and becomes "another woman." "She was so devoted," David writes, "she was so forgetful of herself, and so regardful of the sorrow about her, that I held her in a sort of veneration. . . . She preserved an equable cheerfulness in the midst of her sympathy, which was not the least astonishing part of the change that had come over her" (p. 520). David concludes this observation of the new Mrs. Gummidge: "I left her, when I went away at night, the prop and staff of Mr. Peggotty's affliction; and I could not meditate enough upon the lesson that I read in Mrs. Gummidge, and in the new experience she unfolded to me" (p. 520). When Mr. Peggotty is preparing to emigrate with Emily to Australia, Mrs. Gummidge insists on accompanying them: "I can dig, Dan'l. I can work. I can live hard. I can be loving and patient now—more than you think. . . . I know you think that I am lone and lorn; but deary love, 'tan't so no more!" Mr. Peggotty agrees to take her, of course, and she is "happy" (p. 808). Finally, ten years later, Mr. Peggotty returns to London with the story of the ship's cook who offered to marry her, whom she answered "with a bucket as was standing by," which she "laid . . . over that theer ship's cook's head 'till he sung out for help" (p. 943). This last gesture is a proof both of Mrs. Gummidge's happiness and success in her new useful life—"She's the willinest, the trewest, the honestest-helping woman," Mr. Peggotty says, "as ever draw'd the breath of life" (p. 943)—and of the energy which that new life gives her.

Peggotty's usefulness is both simple and poetic. She is always darning or sewing or working at something. The beautiful particulars of David's first description of her—with her "cheeks and arms so hard and red that I wondered the birds didn't peck her in preference to apples," and her "forefinger . . . roughened by needlework, like a pocket nutmeg-grater" (p. 61)—tell us both how much David loves her and that she is almost metaphysically, definitively useful. When David is locked in his room for biting Mr. Murdstone, it is Peggotty who comes to visit him, to assure him of her love and perform —create—that brilliantly useful act of kissing the keyhole (pp. 110–11). The Murdstones may lock the door on David, but they can't keep Peggotty's love out; and her love is so substantial that it fills, David says, " a vacancy in my heart . . . and I felt toward her something I have never felt for any other human being" (p. 111).

Peggotty knows what being useful means; it means "never leaving" those she loves. And she is resolved to be useful in this way to Clara Copperfield until "I'm too deaf, and too lame, and too blind, and too mumbly for want of teeth, to be of any use at all"—and then, she says, she will "go to my Davy, and ask him to take me in." Without a pause, without even needing to think, knowing immediately even as a child what reward Peggotty's usefulness merits, David answers, "And Peggotty . . . I shall be glad to see you, and I'll make you as welcome as a queen" (p. 164).

When Miss Betsey loses her fortune, Peggotty—a "poor fool," a "simpleton," a "ridiculous creature" Miss Betsey calls her, with "tears of pleasure positively trickling down" her face—volunteers to give Miss Betsey her own money, "because she has got too much of it" (p. 563); and when Mr. Peggotty, utterly forgetful of himself, sets out in search of Emily, Peggotty takes care of him. She is also capable of imaginative usefulness: her wondering—"I really do wonder," she says—about Miss Betsey plants the idea in David's head which later becomes his plan to run away to her from Murdstone and Grinby's. What seems "a fit of wondering" on Peggotty's part—"nonsense" that comes of her "being stupid" (p. 165)—is her thinking ahead for David.

The most important instance of Peggotty's wise usefulness comes in her telling David of the last few hours of his mother's life, discussed earlier in chapter three. She tells David "all that she had to tell" (p. 185), and he dignifies that telling signally by calling it "Peggotty's narration" (p. 186).

Tommy Traddles understands and exhibits a special kind of usefulness, though through most of the novel what shows is his being abused rather than his usefulness. As a boy he is "always being caned" (p. 143) at school, simply because he is the most easily caned boy there. Steerforth abuses him, calling him a "girl" (p. 153) and "Miss Traddles" (p. 154) because of his care for Mr. Mell's feelings; later, Steerforth calls him "soft" (p. 486). Mr. Waterbrook disparages Tommy as

being "nobody's enemy but his own," and "one of those men
who stand in their own light" (p. 432). And Tommy mini-
mizes his own abilities: "I am a plodding kind of fellow," he
says; "I am not a bad compiler . . . but I have no invention at
all" (p. 465). Traddles does manage, however, for himself and
for others who depend on him, even though at the end of the
novel he is "exactly the same simple, unaffected fellow he ever
was" (p. 950)—with "his hair (where he was not bald) . . .
more rebellious than ever" (p. 949). He takes care of Sophie's
family "like a Patriarch" (p. 950), and is a successful lawyer
who will soon become a judge. Despite himself, it seems, he
is a success: "I really have been able," he tells David, "to do
all that I had most at heart" (p. 949).

What Tommy has wanted, of course, has not been for himself—and that is the source of his success. Tommy's talent has
always been his concern for other people. Though Tommy is
caned constantly at Salem House, he is a happy boy—except
when Mr. Mell is fired, and when David's mother dies. His
usefulness is in his selflessness and generosity, in his concern
for the feelings of others. Steerforth is attractive, to David, in
his strength and masculine forwardness—"I still believe
him," says David the narrator, "in virtue of [his] carriage, his
animal spirits, his delightful voice, his handsome face and
figure . . . to have carried a spell with him to which it was a
natural weakness to yield" (p. 157); but that attraction is
indeed a "weakness." David has to learn to appreciate the
very different qualities that are Traddles's. He has to learn to
respect Tommy's simple goodness and selfless ambition, and
to see in his softness a much greater and more useful strength
than Steerforth's. Though Steerforth calls Tommy a "girl"
and "Miss Traddles," laughing at him, David the narrator
very shortly thereafter refers to Mr. Chillup as exhibiting "the
gentleness of a woman" (p. 184), and means obviously to
praise him in doing so: which praise tells us, certainly, that we
are to appreciate Tommy's softness—and its femininity—as
well.[7] The opposite of such softness is Steerforth's male "ride
roughshod . . . win the race" (p. 488) attitude, or Murdstone's
firmness—and his sister's perverse, mean masculinity. Softness is what Dickens rewards at the end of the novel. It is the

source of Tommy's usefulness, and from it comes his personal and public success.[8]

David's usefulness is of an even higher kind than the selfless usefulness of Peggotty and Traddles. David has the "power of doing good" (p. 915), the ability to bring us "delight . . . entertainment . . . instruction" (p. 945)—and that is certainly useful. His power is the power of imagination, the power of the mind: to put the world together, to comprehend it—for the world's sake. Knowledge and wisdom are socially useful; happiness is useful, and creates usefulness in the world.

Let me cite a brief example, not from Dickens, to demonstrate or dramatise the point of wisdom's social usefulness. Several years ago in a course called "Culture as Environment" which I was teaching for the Environmental Studies Program at my university, I had one older lady as a student along with twenty young people. Mrs. Bonar always had something to say in class, and would regularly include with its saying a short bibliography. One afternoon a very bright young man finished jotting down the title Mrs. Bonar had suggested for the day, and then looked at her and said, quite seriously, "Mrs. Bonar, why are you in this class, anyway?" She thought for a minute, and answered:

> After my husband died, I did a lot of volunteer work for a while, but it wasn't very satisfying. I was working as a grey lady or a candy-striper or whatever that's called in the hospital, finally, and one day I just thought, "Now there are plenty of people who can file forms and empty waste baskets—that doesn't take any talent or skill; just energy. I should find something more appropriate to do, that will let me use the sense God gave me." The more I thought about it, the more clear it became: the best thing I could do for society would be to get busy again learning things—all sorts of things! So here I am, back in school.

Mrs. Bonar must have been in her early seventies then—and that's nine years ago. She is still busy learning things, "for society." You can look at what she does—in the Unitarian fellowship or the Grey Panthers or whatever—and see how she is being useful; but that is just what shows most readily. Ann Bonar's real usefulness to society lies in what she does with her mind.

When David is working in Doctor's Commons, a young man

just out of school, he one day suggests to Mr. Spenlow that "we might improve the Commons"—though he "had not the hardihood to suggest to Dora's father that possibly we might even improve the world a little" (p. 540). As David grows into his real profession—as an artist, as an author with a "power of doing good"—he is less timid about wanting "to improve the world." But his method is not just to attack "that part . . . which happened to be nearest," or to assume that the world must automatically get better "if we got up early in the morning, and took off our coats to the work," (p. 540). The most useful thing we can do "to improve the world," according to David and the example he sets, is to be wise and happy and useful in and for it.

We have to be careful with this kind of example, however. In a cultural climate so tuned to arrogance and the assertion of self as ours is, it is important to distinguish between wisdom and ego. There is a big philosophical difference between David's achievement of self—or Ann Bonar's, for that matter —and such egotistical travesties of Romantic philosophy as *Zen and the Art of Motorcycle Maintenance* and *Jonathan Livingston Seagull* or other such popular cult-of-arrogance books.

These minor obscenities will disappear, of course, like graffiti. What survives in literature is always that which despises ego. Things classical are those which summon us or call us together—the Greek root of the word is καλεω, to call, from the Sanskrit KAL or KAR—not those which separate us according to our private and personal levels or degrees. Ego is the arrogant sign of separation, and is its own lonely end. Generosity, selflessness, and all those related social virtues are what, for Dickens and his kind, deserve our thanks and praise. They will survive in our culture—or our culture will not survive! If we learn the classical lesson that David and his life would teach us, Ann Bonar must finally be more famous than What's-his-name Pirsig or Richard Bach—just as Tellus must be better remembered than Croesus.[9]

Dickens knew Milton well, as *Great Expectations* demonstrates. Certainly he knew Milton's representation of the difference between Satan's vain, self-glorying argument that "The mind is its own place, and in itself/Can make a Heav'n of Hell, a Hell of Heav'n,"[10] and what Michael proposes to Adam and Eve as they leave Paradise. Satan carries "Hell within him"[11] but Adam and Eve, if they learn to love, need not "be loath/To leave this Paradise, but shalt possess/A paradise within [them], happier far."[12]

Though David sets out to find if he can be "the hero of [his] own life" (p. 49), and "to get a better understanding of [him]-self, and be a better man" (p. 890), what he accomplishes is social rather than simply personal. Like Wordsworth, who sets out in *The Prelude* "to understand myself,"[13] Dickens assumes in publishing David's life "that the history of a Poet's mind/Is labour not unworthy of regard,"[14] and that in "the story of myself" there is "power to accomplish aught of worth."[15]

The artist is always the social critic, if we will but understand criticism largely enough. Bernard Shaw thought *Little Dorrit* "more seditious than *Das Kapital*"[16] and I would agree. In the same way, *David Copperfield* is more radical, as a novel of social criticism, than *Bleak House* or *Little Dorrit*. Its radicalism is in the way Dickens and David propose to "improve the world": through wisdom, and happiness, and usefulness. "Though men return to servitude as fast/As the tide ebbs," Wordsworth writes at the end of *The Prelude*, "we shall still/ Find solace—knowing what we have learnt to know,/Rich in true happiness"; and for Wordsworth as for Dickens, "true happiness" makes us "joint labourers in the work/ . . . /Of [men's] deliverance, surely yet to come."[17]

NOTES

1. When Dickens began to write his own autobiography, two years earlier, he began his life at this point—according to Forster—rather than "with the beginning of [his] life," as David does. Forster, volume 1, pp. 19–20.

2. The manuscript tells us that the kind of feeling which grows up out of sorrow was important for Dickens. He first has David's sorrow make him "feel very kind towards people, not hate them," then "want to be kind towards people," and finally "feel kinder" (Ms. 115). Dickens rarely revises dialogue—which this is—even in a manuscript so heavily revised as *David Copperfield*'s. The revisions here show him working toward the simplest, most straightforward way of having David say that sorrow breeds kindness.

3. *Biographia Literaria,* chapter 13, p. 263.
4. *Biographia Literaria,* chapter 12, p. 242.
5. For Coleridge, the secondary imagination—what I have been referring to here—would become "the infinite I Am" if ever it achieved the idealization and completion which it seeks. It would become the primary imagination, the life force or source of life itself.
6. To memorialize the Lord Somebody or other—about this "mad world" —is surely to memorialize God. See *Noah's Arkitecture*, pp. 71–75 for a full argument of this point.
7. Joe Gargery has this same grace, and lays his hand on Pip's shoulder "with the touch of a woman" (p. 168). And "softening"—as Joel Brattin has pointed out to me—is an important theme throughout *Great Expectations.*
8. Dickens worked very carefully with Steerforth's responses to Traddles. In the Salem House scene, he first calls Tommy "stupid" in the manuscript, and this is then changed to "you girl"; his reference to Tommy as "Miss Traddles" in an interlinear addition (Ms. 90). When David tells Steerforth of Tommy's being in London, Dickens works the line through three times before he has Steerforth call Traddles "soft" (Ms. 303).
9. Cf. Herodotus, *The Histories* (Penguin edition), p. 51.
10. *Paradise Lost*, book 1, lines 254–55.
11. *Paradise Lost,* book 4, line 20.
12. *Paradise Lost,* book 12, lines 585–87.
13. *The Prelude,* book 1, line 627.
14. *The Prelude,* book 14, lines 413–14.
15. *The Prelude,* book 14, lines 389–91.
16. George Bernard Shaw, foreword to *Great Expectations* (1937).
17. *The Prelude,* book 14, lines 435–39 and 441–43.

CHAPTER 6

"Talk to me of love! ... Talk to me of fiery dragons!"

That "our deliverance" is "yet to come" is sure for Dickens in that it hasn't come yet. Wordsworth's *Prelude* was published by the poet's widow in 1850; *David Copperfield*, finished in October of that same year, comes in the middle of Dickens's career. He wrote seven novels before *David Copperfield*, and seven more between 1850 and his death twenty years later. These last seven novels, beginning with *Bleak House*, are generally recognized as his most serious and comprehensive novels of social criticism. This is true, in a sense; but by the time he gets to *Our Mutual Friend*, in 1863, that this world is not yet perfect is no longer as frustrating for him as it once was.

What frees him from the kind of frustration and rage that so often marks novels like *Bleak House, Hard Times, Little Dorrit,* and *A Tale of Two Cities* is that he is more sure, in *Our Mutual Friend*, of the general effectiveness of the "power of knowledge; the power derivable from ... perfect comprehension" (p. 241), and of the "power" love has "of doing good to others" (p. 747). He seems sure that the order of the mind can solve the chaos of the world in which we live, and that the kind of sympathetic understanding which he calls wisdom is legitimately an end in itself. He has also determined—proved to his own imaginative satisfaction—that truth will out, that reality can't forever be hidden or disguised. In *David Copperfield*, Agnes has a "hope that simple love and truth will be strong in the end," a "hope that real love and truth are stronger in the end than any evil or misfortune in the world" (DC, p. 572). In a very large and sure way, *Our Mutual Friend* is Dickens's optimistic philosophical response to that hope.

Our Mutual Friend is a complex and difficult book. It seems to begin several times in its opening chapters. First we are introduced to Gaffer Hexam and Lizzie, on the river—and a "pardner" who is not a "pardner" (p. 47), and a body in tow. Then in chapter 2 we meet the Veneerings and their kind—friends who are not friends—and Mortimer Lightwood and Eugene Wrayburn and the story of "the Man from Somewhere." In chapter 3 we meet Charley Hexam, and Julius Handford—who obviously isn't Julius Handford. In chapter 4 we meet the Wilfer family—including Bella, the "widow who was never married" (p. 80)—and John Rokesmith. In chapter 5 we meet the Boffins and Silas Wegg, the "literary man" who is not a literary man. What's the focus? What—or who—is this novel about? How many novels is Dickens writing?

But this multiple opening isn't all of the novel's multiplicity or complexity. Gaffer Hexam introduces us to the Six Jolly Fellowship-Porters, and his erstwhile partner brings in his daughter Pleasant and her trade in sailors. Lizzie takes us to Jenny Wren and her father, and then to Mr. Riah. Charley Hexam goes to Bradley Headstone's school, and Bradley's school introduces Miss Peecher and Mary Anne. The Veneerings introduce the world of society, and a comic extendibility that produces "a Member, an Engineer, a Payer-Off of the National Debt, a Poem on Shakespeare, a Grievance, and a Public Office," (p. 49) as well as Boots and Brewer and an unlimited supply of "Buffers" (pp. 53 ff.). The Wilfers, curiously, introduce us to nobody new except Rokesmith, whom we have already met in other ways in each of the three preceding chapters, and George Sampson, who doesn't appear in the flesh—except as a pair of legs (p. 152)—for another fifty-one chapters. Through the Boffins we meet the Milveys, Betty Higden, little Johnny, and Mr. Sloppy; through Wegg we meet Mr. Venus—and the baby in the bottle and a dozen other curiosities.

The world of *Our Mutual Friend* is large and "warious" (p. 121). Reading it we feel like Noddy Boffin, perhaps, having *The Decline and Fall of the Roman Empire* read to him: it would help, we think, to have a program, or a cast of characters, or an index of some kind. But no such aid would be very useful, since people change. First there's Julius Handford who is

John Rokesmith who is John Harmon. Then there are Alfred
Lammle and Sophronia Akersham, who fool each other, and
together—clever married fools—set out to fool the rest of
society. Podsnap fools himself—and Podsnappery, alas, fools
almost all of us. And the Veneerings: they had us all fooled,
too, until the end. Noddy Boffin and Henrietta, once old
Harmon's servants, become fashionable people for a while,
and Noddy pretends to become a miser. Bradley Headstone
is always "repressing himself" (p. 345) in order to perform his
duties, while his pupil, Charley, is busy "raising" himself "in
the scale of society" (p. 343). Society would call his sister a
"female waterman" and a "factory girl," but Twemlow calls
her a "lady" (p. 891). Fascination Fledgeby, born as a result
of a pecuniary miscarriage (p. 320), hides behind Mr. Riah,
who has to pretend to be a stereoptypical Jew though he is in
fact a "fairy godmother." Jenny Wren, who for a while calls
Mr. Riah "Mr. Wolf" (p. 794), is really Fanny Cleaver, and Mr.
Dolls is not her "bad child" but her father—whose name is
Mr. Cleaver, presumably. Pa Wilfer won't claim his name—
Reginald—but writes himself "R. Wilfer"; Dickens volunteers
eleven alternate "christian names" for Pa, though the one
most people call him by is "Rumty" (pp. 75–76). Twemlow is
taken for Veneering at a party, and Lady Tippins's late husband was "knighted in mistake for somebody else" (p. 164).
Sloppy—who has no fuller name—"do the police in different
voices" (p. 246), and disguises himself "in fantail hat and
velveteen smalls" as the "Demon of Unrest" (p. 850).

In creating this vast complex of changing characters Dickens makes his most complete and realistic representation of
"this changing world" (OT, p. 476). It deserves—needs, in
fact—both an "Analytical Chemist" (p. 51) and someone
skilled in "articulating" (p. 126) to "fit together . . . the whole
framework of society" (p. 540).[1] But a butler called "the
Analytical" and a sad taxidermist with a "knowledge of
Anatomy" (p. 128) can't save the world, even the world of a
novel. They aren't meant for that; rather, they are symbolic
characters whose roles tell us, as readers, how Dickens would
save the world and how he would instruct us toward that end.

As the Analytical introduces his symbolic motif at the Ve-

neerings' house, so the process of analysis in the novel begins
there, with a highly satirical look at "Society" and "what it's
made of" (p. 52). In his representation of Podsnap and the
devotees of Podsnappery Dickens creates caricatures and
stereotypes—"specimen," rather than characters. His excuse
for this is that he knows the Veneerings, Lady Tippins, and
their kind to be false. His critical response to them is like
David's response to Jane Murdstone once he is sure he knows
her, and it shows in the narrative tone and technique, as
Dickens laughs at them. The most interesting members of
Podsnap's world are the Lammles; we see behind their cover
of class, and discover that they have passions—which won't
stereotype—as well as cunning. The others, however, are
reducible, and the narrative voice indulges in caricature in
presenting them to us as little more than comically well-
dressed dolls or puppets.

But they aren't Thackeray's pathetically famous puppets,
characters reduced to puppetry by their author's cynical piety.
Dickens's puppets are recognizably created as puppets by the
attitude of the narrator, in a brilliant act of metaphysical judgment. Dickens knows Podsnap's pompous stupidity and
Veneering's falseness; his eye for the "peculiarities and oddities" of our race is even more accurate than usual here, and
he has caught them all in that "net" of comprehension which
David spoke of needing as a boy (DC, p. 70). Dickens know
them, and knows their falseness: like Jenny Wren, he says to
them, "*I* know your tricks and manners" (p. 292 and elsewhere). He dehumanizes them by reducing them to stereotypes, and insists, then, that the stereotypes are their symbolic
meanings.

What they mean is what ties them into the novel's larger
realism. Their gestures are exaggerated, but their meaning
isn't: the narrator convinces us that he sees them as they really
are, and that his satiric representation of them is accurate. His
excuse for manipulating them like puppets is that they don't
measure up to humanity. He reduces them with his jokes—
just as Milton's God reduces Satan—because their evil is no
longer a threat to him. Fraud and treachery, as intellectual
sins, are reduced to "mischief"—to bathetically comic mis-

uses of the mind. What Podsnap and Veneering mean, now, is less than human meaning; the way they act proves this, and justifies Dickens's satiric judgment of them.

For Dickens, human reality must have meaning. Like Browning, he assumes always that this world "means intensely," and because of what meaning is, even that it "means good"; and in almost literal ways, by the time he gets to *Our Mutual Friend* and especially *Edwin Drood,* Dickens would say with Browning that "to find its meaning is my meat and drink."[2]

Dickens treats the false world of negative meaning satirically because there is no other way he can treat it. When he turns to the more human or potentially human characters in the novel, however, he identifies them individually, in terms of their personality and values. Values, for Dickens, are metaphysical rather than moral qualities. Thus Bella Wilfer, though she is a wilful and "mercenary wretch" from the beginning, is attractive because she *is* wilful and passionate and full of energy. Thus Eugene Wrayburn is important because he knows what Society is, and objects to it; though Eugene refuses to know himself, Dickens trusts him, metaphysically, because he resists the falseness of the world around him. And Bradley Headstone, though he is introduced reductively, dehumanized in his "decent black coat and waistcoat, and decent white shirt, and decent formal black tie" and his ability to do "almost anything mechanically" (p. 266), is a man of passion, and therefore is interesting to Dickens. Bradley has a "passionate" self, and knows it; he spends his days "watching and repressing it" (p. 345).

These three are perhaps the most important characters in *Our Mutual Friend*—except for Mortimer. But Mortimer's attitudes and interests are different from theirs, and his role in the novel is different. His very being is different from theirs, and from almost everybody else's in Dickens's world. His only close kinsmen are David and, in *Edwin Drood,* Mr. Grewgious and whoever Datchery is. We will consider Mortimer in the next chapter.

I want us first to consider Bella and Eugene. In so doing we will lose sight, for the moment, of the large complex world in which they live and from which we extract them in order to look at their development. But both Bella and Eugene are extractable—and that, perhaps, is the first critical point to be made. Neither Bella nor Eugene is attached to the world at the beginning of the novel: Bella because she thinks only of herself and ignores the world, Eugene because he refuses to assert or claim a self in the world.

Bella's egotistical isolation from the world is represented first by her self-proclaimed widowhood, and then by her interest in money. That widowhood can mean isolation may have come to Dickens from the impact of Queen Victoria's prolonged seclusion after Albert's death. Albert died in December of 1861; despite appeals and admonitions from all quarters, the Queen did not appear in public for three years thereafter. In June of 1864, when she made her reappearance, the first monthly number of *Our Mutual Friend*—with Bella's widowhood established in chapter 4—was several weeks old. Certainly Dickens's audience would have felt the significance of Bella's calling herself a widow, and dressing in black, and responding to the Boffins's first invitation to visit them, "I doubt if I have the inclination to go out at all" (p. 154); they were thoroughly upset with what widowhood had come to mean to Victoria.

Bella's absurd comic retreat into widowhood has to be wrong, because retreat is wrong, for Dickens; it is worse because in retreat she indulges her selfish desires. Knowing nothing of the world, she decides what its "realities" are, and pursues them. She values possession—not just "money, but . . . what it will buy" (p. 374)—more than relation. "Talk to me of love!" she says; "Talk to me of fiery dragons! But talk to me of poverty and wealth, and there indeed we touch upon realities" (p. 376).

When Bella's climactic scene with Noddy Boffin and John Rokesmith comes, and Rokesmith talks of love, Noddy picks up Bella's idea that love is something that belongs in fairy tales and children's stories, and teases her with it. He translates Rokesmith's promise to "win her affections and possess her heart" into "Mew says the cat, Quack-quack says the duck, Bow-wow-wow says the dog!" and contrasts that with the

grown-up reality of "Money" (p. 660). Bella knows how
wrong this is, and claims in response to Mr. Boffin that Rokesmith's love, not money, is what has real value or "worth" (pp.
662, 664). Then, continuing her new appreciation of "fancy,"
she names her Pa "the Knave of Wilfers" (p. 682).

The narrative voice responds to the change in Bella by
creating a marvellously comic fantasy for her and John and Pa
on the day of her wedding. Bella and John have "an ethereal
air of happiness" about them as they walk toward the church
in Greenwich—and that air is so real that it seems "wafted up
from the earth, and [draws] after them a gruff and glum old
pensioner." This pensioner—with "two wooden legs"—
quickly becomes a character called "Gruff and Glum," and we
are told that Bella's brilliance and beauty have "floated him"
out of a "harbour of everlasting mud" (p. 731) in which he
has long been sunk. During the wedding itself Pa is afraid that
Mrs. Wilfer may arrive to spoil everything; the narrator describes Pa's fears as of her coming "in a car and griffins, like
the spiteful Fairy" (p. 732). But Bella dispatches a letter to her
mother—upon which "the queen's countenance" looks more
than naturally "benign"—and declares that Pa is now "safe,
and will never be taken alive" (p. 733).

The narrator's fantasy isn't over, however, with this act;
"the marriage dinner was the crowning success" (p. 734), he
says—and he makes it so, magically and alchemically. The
dinner is presided over by a waiter who is playfully but unre-
lentingly transformed into "the Archbishop of Greenwich"; it
begins with "specimens of all the fishes that swam in the sea,"
and "samples of the fishes of diverse colours that made a
speech in the Arabian Nights," and continues through dishes
"seasoned with Bliss," accompanied by "golden drinks [that]
had been bottled in the golden age" (p. 735). Under the
influence of such narrative exuberance, Pa forgets his usual
self-effacing manner and boldly makes a heady speech addressed to "Gentlemen—and Bella and John" (p. 737), and
dedicated to the newly-weds' happiness. At the end of the
chapter, as John and Bella turn homeward, the path they
follow is made "rosy" by "the gracious sun," and the fantasy
is completed with an appeal to the "bright old song . . . that

O 'tis love, 'tis love, 'tis love, that makes the world go around"
(p. 738).

The reason for all of this fantastic celebration is Bella's
conversion, which the narrator is now certain of, from his
reading of her responses to love and money. Bella proves him
right, of course. She was only "giddy for want of some sustaining purpose" (pp. 587–88); her new self is her "natural"
self (p. 738). Loving John, she has no desire to be rich, except
in love (pp. 747, 751, 825), and being in love she finds that
reality is more on the side of fiery dragons than she thought:

> "Dear John, your wishes are as real to me as the wishes in the
> Fairy story, that were fulfilled as soon as spoken. Wish me every-
> thing that you can ever wish for the woman you dearly love, and
> I have as good as got it, John. I have better than got it, John."
> (748)

Bella has learned, obviously, to value love—and more, she has
learned both that love is a firm reality and that love makes
dreams come true: that what the imagination creates is real
and true, and that the imagination's reality and truth make her
happy.

Again, such happiness is radiant. At Greenwich, Bella's face
gives her away as a newly-wed, she says, "because I look so
happy" (p. 737). To John, she is "like a bright light in the
house," the source of which is her "being inspired by her
affection" (p. 750)—and this inspiration, then, makes her "serious" (p. 751) as she looks at the world around her. The new
Bella is tested, tried, proved, and in terms of value and worth
she turns out to be "true golden gold at heart" (p. 843). The
generous and radiant ways of her golden heart are her "natural ways" (p. 880), we are told: and such a nature, discovered,
vindicates the narrator's partiality to her from the beginning.
Bella, "the boofer lady," may well start to change the world.

Eugene begins the novel in the midst of Society, "buried
alive in the back of his chair" (p. 53) at the Veneerings' dinner
party. The world that assembles itself at "Stucconia" (pp.
163, 165) is disgusting to him, and he withdraws, morbidly.
Though the troubles of the Man from Somewhere and his
sister "touch" him as Mortimer tells their story, Lady Tippins's remark about her "lovers" and the cosy courting of the

Lammles-to-be make him suicidal again: "his gloom deepens
to that degree that he trifles quite ferociously with his dessert-
knife" (p. 57).

Because his profession as a barrister has been "forced upon
[him]," Eugene can only "hate" it. He has been seven years
in this calling, and to date "has had no business at all, and
never shall have any" (pp. 61–62). He despises the idea of
"energy" as "parrot gabble" (p. 62), and protests "on principle" (p. 138) against the busy bee as a "tyrannical humbug"
(p. 139). Because his father has tried to force a wife—"with
some money, of course" (p. 193)—upon him as well as a
profession, Eugene professes himself "bored" by the idea of
matrimony (p. 194). Rejecting society, he protests against
"the unlimited monotony of one's fellow-creatures" (p. 192).

Given what we have seen of Society, Eugene's withdrawal
is understandable, of course; like Bella's, however, it is still
wrong. It is wrong because it is irresponsible—because it
makes him irresponsible. As a defense against society, Eugene
refuses to assert a self, and denies any knowledge of himself.
But no matter how bad or mad the world is, Dickens accepts
no excuse for personal irresponsibility. Responsibility is the
core of his Romantic optimism. And responsibility requires
self-knowledge: without it, I can't *promise for myself*—which is
what the word responsibility says I must do.

When Mortimer questions Eugene about his interest in
Lizzie, after her brother and Bradley Headstone have visited
them, Eugene answers that he has no interest in her because
he has no interests: that he has no "designs" of any kind upon
her because he is "incapable of designs" (p. 348)—and that
he is "incapable of designs" because he doesn't know where
he is going, or what he is doing, or who he is. In answer to
Mortimer's questions on these points, he refers his friend to
"the troublesome conundrum long abandoned," the riddle of
himself. "Eugene Wrayburn," he says, and taps his forehead
and breast to indicate the subject: "Riddle-me, riddle-me-ree,
perhaps you can't tell me what this may be?—No, upon my life
I can't. I give it up!" (p. 349).

At the beginning of this chapter Mortimer has accused Eugene of "withholding something" from him. Eugene's re-

sponse is somewhat evasive. "I don't know," he says, because "I know less about myself than about most people in the world" (p. 338).

> "You must take your friend as he is. You know what I am, my dear Mortimer. You know how dreadfully susceptible I am to boredom. You know that when I became enough of a man to find myself an embodied conundrum, I bored myself to the last degree by trying to find out what I meant. You know that at length I gave it up, and declined to guess any more. Then how can I possibly give you the answer that I have not discovered? The old nursery form runs, 'Riddle-me, riddle-me-ree, p'raps you can't tell me what this may be?' My reply runs, 'No. Upon my life I can't.' " (338–39).

Though Mortimer takes this answer as "true to his own knowledge of" Eugene, and thus not "mere evasion" (p. 339), he knows it to be the answer of an "utterly careless" person who lives and acts with "reckless indifference" (p. 339).

Eugene is not evading Mortimer directly; rather, he is evading himself, as his repeated recourse to the "riddle" indicates. That the handy riddle is an attempt at self-evasion is underscored by his choice of a relative pronoun for himself. In questioning "what" rather than "who" he may be, he tries ironically to dehumanize himself and his human responsibility. For Dickens, however, to be so wilfully or negligently ignorant of oneself is culpable. Though Mortimer tries here to excuse Eugene, and Lizzie would never blame him for anything, Eugene hurts them both—his first, best friend and the woman who loves him—by this irresponsibility to and for himself.

Between the two halves of this scene of Eugene's with Mortimer comes the visit Charley and his schoolmaster pay to them. As Mortimer finishes his questioning of his aimless friend—Eugene has proposed "smoking," ironically, as a means to clarification or "enlightment" of the subject—Eugene aims small clods of dirt "dexterously" and "with great precision" at a mark. Then two "wanderers" enter the court beneath their window, and Eugene takes aim at one of them. Idly, he narrates his action: "On the hat of wanderer number two, the shorter one, I drop this pellet. Hitting him on the hat, I smoke serenely, and become absorbed in contemplation of

the sky" (p. 340). The accuracy of his aim in this small symbolic action belies his claim to have no "designs," and his
elaborate pretence to innocence is the mark of his irresponsibility. Eugene is amused, however, by his game, and plans
"when they emerge" to "bring them both down"—and to
underline the self-deception involved in Eugene's declared
ignorance of himself, the narrator notes that he has "prepared two pellets for the purpose" (p. 340).

In the scene that follows Eugene does bring both "wanderers" down. Charley he simply ignores; with the "cruel" wit
and "cold disdain" (p. 345) of the social class he claims to
despise, he brutalizes Bradley with condescension. At the climax of the scene, when Bradley accuses Eugene of having
"cast insinuations at [his] bringing-up," Eugene answers,
"how [can I] cast stones that were never in my hand" (p. 346).
The "two pellets" "prepared . . . for the purpose" echo in this
false disclaimer, telling us that Eugene lies to others as well
as to himself. His joke, then, that he is "doing all [he] can
towards self-improvement" (p. 348) is not a joke at all.

Eugene knows, of course, what he is doing; but he won't be
serious, won't take himself seriously. Dickens has created
characters before who are knowingly irresponsible like Eugene is—and the knowing, however small or weak it is, is what
saves them. What seems to make Eugene redeemable is that
from the beginning of his interest in Lizzie he feels "guilty"
(p. 212)—because however much he protests that he is "in a
ridiculous humour," he knows just as Mortimer does that he
is being "negligent and reckless" (p. 213).

The first few times the novel focuses on Eugene the same
elements of information and personality appear: his claim not
to know himself, his carelessness and his inability to be serious for more than a moment, his boredom with everything,
and his awful sense of his own uselessness. When he visits
Lizzie at Jenny Wren's house, Jenny greets him saying, "Mr.
Eugene Wrayburn, ain't it?" and he replies, typically, "So I
am told." She says, "You may come in, if you're good," and
he answers, "I am not good . . . but I'll come in" (p. 284). "I
am a bad idle dog," he says, and Jenny asks pertinently,
"Then why don't you reform and be a good dog?" He re-

sponds, "Because, my dear . . . there's nobody who makes it worth my while" (p. 285). When he proposes "to be of some use" to Lizzie—"which I never was in this world, and never shall be on any other occasion"—he has the "appearance of earnestness, complete conviction . . . generous and unselfish interest"; but this is only a "change . . . for the moment," a "passing appearance" (p. 286). The "appearance of openness, trustfulness, unsuspecting generosity, in his words and manner" (p. 288) lingers or returns, however, and Lizzie accepts his offer. Leaving, he pauses "to light another cigar"—"and possibly to ask himself what he was doing." But the narrator is sceptical of his finding an answer to his question, and comments, "Who knows what he is doing, who is careless what he does!" (p. 291).

The next time Eugene encounters Lizzie she is with Mr. Riah. As the three of them walk together, Eugene acts his usual part, "going on at her side, so gaily, regardless" of everything; but "for all his seeming levity and carelessness, he knew whatever he chose to know of the thoughts of her heart" (p. 464). When he and Mr. Riah have walked Lizzie home, they part. "I give you good night," says Mr. Riah, "and I wish you were not so thoughtless." Eugene answers, rejecting the criticism, "I give you good night, and I wish you were not so thoughtful" (p. 465).

> But now, that his part was played out for the evening . . . he was thoughtful himself. "How did Lightwood's catechism run?" he murmered, as he stopped to light his cigar. "What is to come of it? What are you doing? Where are you going? We shall soon know now. Ah!" (465)

Lizzie also urges Eugene to be thoughtful. When they meet alongside the river, Lizzie appeals to his "better nature" (p. 760), and urges him to "think now, think now" (p. 761). Eugene admits that he has lied to her, and again tells her his one truth, "I am not good" (p. 760). He confesses too, that the "cursed carelessness" which he practices in dealing with the rest of the world won't help him with her. Because she insists on it, he promises to leave her alone from this night forward; but as soon as Lizzie is gone he comes to the "reckless conclusion" to "try her again" (p. 765).

Eugene has no opportunity to "try her again," of course. After Bradley's attack on him, he lies near death for days. Jenny is sent for, because he wants her: he remembers her dreams of birds and flowers, and of "long bright slanting rows of children who used to bring [her] ease and rest" (p. 806). She tells him that she "never sees them now," because she is "hardly ever in pain now" (p. 807).

> "It was a pretty fancy," said Eugene.
> "But I have heard my birds sing," cried the little creature, "and I have smelt the flowers. Yes, indeed I have! And both were most beautiful and most Divine!"
> "Stay and help to nurse me," said Eugene, quietly. "I should like you to have the fancy, here, before I die."
> She touched his lips with her hand, and shaded her eyes with that same hand as she went back to her . . . little low song. He heard the song with evident pleasure. (807).

Jenny's answer to Eugene here is like her answer to him when first we hear of her "fancies," early in the novel:

> "I wonder how it happens that when I am work, work, working here, all alone in the summer-time, I smell flowers."
> "As a commonplace individual, I should say," Eugene suggested languidly—for he was growing weary of [Jenny] . . .—"that you smell flowers because you *do* smell flowers."
> "No I don't," said the little creature. . . . "And yet as I sit at work, I smell miles of flowers." (289)

Like Bella, Eugene has to learn that "fancies" are—or can be —real. He asks for Jenny's "fancy," of seeing children or smelling flowers or hearing birds sing, and she gives him his wish in reality, singing Jenny Wren's "little low song" which he hears "with evident pleasure" (p. 807).

Eugene's next problem is related to his recklessness and carelessness and lack of concentration. Near death, he keeps losing consciousness. He refers to this pathetically as his "wandering away" (pp. 807 ff.), and fears that he will "lose [him]self again" in such wanderings. He wants to say something to Mortimer, but can't focus his attention long enough to say it. Finally Jenny says it for him: "Wife." Just as she made her "fancy" real for him, she gives Eugene "the right word" (p. 811) that will make his own fancy—his love for Lizzie—real as well.

Eugene's love for Lizzie saves him. When Mortimer returns to Eugene's bedside with her, he asks, "Is he conscious, Jenny?" and Eugene answers for himself, "He is conscious, Jenny"; and he adds—as self-assertion—"He knows his wife" (p. 812). As he begins to recover, he realizes what her love for him can do: "Out of your compassion for me," he says, "you make so much of me" (p. (824). And when he determines, then, to "turn to in earnest" (p. 885), he does so with a "mine of purpose and energy" (p. 825) and with Lizzie by his side. Teasing, testing, he tells Mortimer that he and Lizzie may run away from this real world, to someplace like Mr. Micawber's Australia: "I have had an idea . . . of taking myself and my wife to one of the colonies, and working at my vocation there." Mortimer answers, cautiously, "I should be lost without you, Eugene; but you may be right." "Emphatically," with "a lively —almost angry—flash," Eugene responds, "No. . . . Not right. Wrong!" (p. 885). He is full of "animation" now, in committing himself to work—to "fight it out"—in and for this world.

His decision not to run away completes Eugene's salvation. His determination to stay in this world and confront it with the justness and honor of his new life makes him radiant, and makes him whole again:

> The glow that shone upon him . . . so irradiated his features that he looked, for the time, as though he had never been mutilated. (886)

At the end, Eugene is rewarded as few characters in Dickens's world ever are: he and Mortimer, we are told, "discoursed of the future"—in which we should expect them to do something both energetic and wise.

Eugene's success is the happy achievement of self-determination, Bella's the miracle of self-discovery. Bradley Headstone, however, begins his career in *Our Mutual Friend* very differently. When we meet him, he has already determined what his public self must be: the "decent" (p. 266) self of a "highly certificated stipendiary schoolmaster" (p. 265), which will hide his origin. He has already discovered his private or personal self, also, and has found it too "animal" and "fiery" not to need repression (p. 267).

Bella begins the novel separated from the world by her silly

selfishness; in the end, she becomes "serious" (p. 751) and so
"rich" in love that she may have "a great power of doing good
to others" (p. 747). At first Eugene, too, separates himself
from the world—from Society—because he sees and abhors
its falseness; in the end he overcomes his alienation, and can
speak enthusiastically of "turning to in earnest" and "working
at [his] vocation" (p. 885) in the world. Bradley, however, sets
out as a very young man to make himself acceptable to the
world on its terms; as a consequence, he becomes much more
deeply and dangerously alienated than either Eugene or
Bella.

Bella's selfishness is only "surface," the result of her being
"spoilt" (p. 843)—and she knows that it is wrong. Eugene
sees Society itself as spoil, as contamination, and resists it to
keep from being spoiled by it. But Bradley submits himself—
"mechanically" (p. 266)—to what the world wants of him, and
consciously, intentionally suppresses and disguises his nature
and personality in order to be acceptable to it. In so doing,
he becomes dangerously alienated. He does violence to himself—and reflexively, then, becomes himself violent.

Both Eugene and Bella are saved and made responsible by
love. Love "proves" Bella "true golden gold" (p. 843), and
it puts Eugene on "the right course for a true man" (p. 812).
The experience of love does something very different to
Bradley—or, rather, what Bradley experiences in his attraction to Lizzie is not love, but passionate obsession to possess
her, and his passion destroys him. In order to become what
Society would call respectable and win respectability's prizes,
Bradley has tried all his poor life to "suppress" and "restrain"
his passionate nature (p. 396): has felt himself "obliged habit-
ually to keep . . . down" what he feels (p. 400) in order someday to possess what he wants. But "smouldering natures" like
his will—must—someday "burst into flame" (p. 396), Dickens
argues; we must recognize the terrible reality of such individual, personal explosions, and not think of them as but like the
breathings of "fiery dragons." One of Jenny's many fancies is
that Bradley may "take fire and blow up" (p. 402)—and like
her other imaginings, this one too comes true.

We see the truth of Bradley's passion in the violence of his gesture in the churchyard at St. Peter's in Leadenhall, when he asks Lizzie to marry him. The gesture is first simply an unspecified "passionate action of his hands" (p. 452); his repetition of "that former action of his hands" is described figuratively as "like flinging his heart's blood down before her in drops upon the pavement-stones" (p. 453).[3] Next Bradley is described as having "laid his hand upon a piece of the coping of the burial-ground enclosure," and of having "again grapsed the stone" (p. 454), and then of having "wrenched" the stone loose, so that the "powdered mortar . . . rattled on the pavement" (p. 455). Finally the gesture is completed— made meaningful—in his "bringing his clenched hand down upon the stone with a force that laid the knuckles raw and bleeding" (p. 456).

Bradley stands, "holding out his smeared hand as if it held some weapon and had just struck a mortal blow" (p. 456). The blood, however, is Bradley's own, and what the gesture means is self-destructive violence. The image of his bloody hand foreshadows his attack on Eugene, of course; but more literally it signifies Bradley's own destruction. It means the same thing that his violent nosebleeds and his fit of "biting and knocking about him" (p. 821) mean: Bradley is destroying himself from within. His passion is destroying him—as Jenny fancied it would.

Bradley dies, having failed in his attempt to love. He doesn't combust spontaneously, however; he commits suicide. He dies with his accuser, Rogue Riderhood: the man in whose image he committed his crime. Rogue is the novel's first false man: a false friend, a false "pardner" (p. 46). Bradley's last irony, as a passionate man, is that he dies embracing —in an "iron ring" (p. 874)—the man he chose as his double, the one man in the novel who has proved himself to be essentially evil. Thus in his death Bradley judges himself.

The first thing Eugene does after the attack by the river is to make Mortimer promise not to accuse or prosecute Bradley, for fear of harming Lizzie's reputation: "It is not the schoolmaster, Bradley Headstone," he says over and over (p. 808), negating—refusing, rejecting—the fact and consequences of Bradley's crime. Then Bradley, the failed lover and violent man—his own accuser, prosecutor, and judge—murders Bradley. Eugene, loving Lizzie and determining to be a responsible man in the world, looks "for the time," at least, "as though he had never been mutilated" (p. 886): as though love has made him whole.

Sitting in the Lock House at Plashwater Mill with Rogue Riderhood, Bradley's face loses its light, "turning whiter and whiter as if it were being overspread with ashes" (p. 872). Bella, however, turns "true golden gold" (p. 844), and the "pretty" and "promising" and "hopeful picter" she makes is such that it seems "as if [old Harmon's] money had turned bright again . . . and was at last beginning to sparkle in the sunlight" (p. 849). Eugene, too, becomes radiant with the light of love: when he speaks of Lizzie, a "glow . . . irradiated his features" (p. 886). Dickens knows that "love" is often no more than a "trite expression quite sufficiently discussed" (p. 396); but he is not afraid of or embarrassed by the repetitious nature of the "bright old song . . . that "O 'tis love, 'tis love, 'tis love, that makes the world go round" (p. 738). He would have us learn that active, radiant truth, and believe it.

NOTES

1. Nancy A. Metz has also written about analysis and articulation as the main critical motifs in this novel; see her essay, "The Artistic Reclamation of Waste in *Our Mutual Friend,*" in *Nineteenth Century Fiction.*
2. Robert Browning, "Fra Lippo Lippi," lines 314–15. For *Edwin Drood,* see chapter IX below.
3. Cf. John Jasper's repetition of this gesture in his passionate declaration of his perverse desire for Rosa Bud in *Edwin Drood* (p. 231).

CHAPTER 7

"What is life but learning?"

The first two-thirds of *Pickwick Papers* is comic in a way that nothing in all of Dickens's works ever is again. What Dickens sees as the world in 1836 doesn't need to be taken seriously, so he can treat both what goes on and the way those goings on are reported to us as innocent entertainment. After Mr. Pickwick—and Dickens with him—learns what the world is really like, in chapter 45, that kind of comedy disappears forever. When Dickens creates simple comic scenes thereafter, they are usually either sentimental or satiric: his comedy comes either from his closing his eyes to the real world or from his ironic manipulation of it. Sentimental comedy is a denial of the world, satiric comedy is a rejection of it.

Sometimes, however, Dickens creates a kind of transcendent comedy which is fully engaged with the real world—knows it and takes it seriously—but still can treat it playfully and humorously. Perhaps, remembering my argument in chapter 4 above, you will let me explain this transcendent comedy by reference to the form it most resembles: tragedy. Dicken's greatest, most complete tragedy is *David Copperfield; Our Mutual Friend* and *Edwin Drood* are, as I hope to persuade you in these last three chapters, remarkably like it.

Our Mutual Friend is a serious novel, to be sure; but the heavy and aggressive rhetoric of *Bleak House* and *Hard Times* appears only once in its pages, in two paragraphs late in the novel dedicated to "my lords and gentlemen and honourable boards," professionally busy at their "dust-shovelling and cinder-raking" (pp. 565–66); otherwise this novel doesn't threaten us with "the Writing on the Wall" (HT, p. 313) or want to blow us up (BH, pp. 55, 169, 307, 357, 425, 432, 512,

517, 612, 701, 779). The closest we get to spontaneous combustion here is Bradley Headstone's high blood pressure and
his violent nose-bleeds—which are symptomatic of Bradley's
personal troubles, not symbols of the world's disease.[1]

But *Our Mutual Friend* is a novel of social criticism, and in
the same way that *David Copperfield* is. Like David's novel, it
looks toward our "deliverance": it defines deliverance in
terms of the function of the imagination, which will teach us
to be wise and happy and useful in the world.[2] But there is no
artist-figure here, like David; the chief story-teller in *Our Mutual Friend* is a young lawyer named Mortimer Lightwood,
who has "founded himself upon" his friend Eugene Wrayburn (p. 337)—and for most of the novel Eugene is lost and
ignorant of himself (pp. 338–39).

In *Bleak House*, the novel Dickens wrote immediately following *David Copperfield*, the narration is divided between Esther
Summerson, a self-effacing young woman who worries always
as she writes about what she does and doesn't know, and an
aggressively omniscient narrator who shows us the world always in terms of what it means, insisting on our seeing it as
he sees it. If we ask ourselves how *Bleak House*, so described,
relates to *David Copperfield*, the answer we get is simple but
revealing. The omniscient narrator's domineering omniscience comes from what David the narrator has learned, for
Dickens, from his successful imaginative comprehension of
the world; and Esther is Dickens's recreation of David the
character. But the narrator of *Bleak House* doesn't sound at all
like David the narrator, and though Esther is always trying to
"understand" things, and has "rather a noticing way" (p. 62),
she is not an artist. She professes herself to be singularly
unimaginative—"I know I am not clever," she says, beginning
her "portion of these pages" (p. 62); "I have not by any means
a quick understanding" (p. 63). And having been raised by an
aunt who wishes her niece had never been born—rather than
Miss Betsey, who wanted a niece—Esther sets out in this
world having to create herself psychologically as well as come
to understand herself. She needs to find a place for herself in
the world—"to win some love to myself" (p. 65) as she says
—before she can undertake to comprehend it.

Our Mutual Friend seems at first to be related to *David Copperfield* in a similarly limited way. Like Esther, the David figure in *Our Mutual Friend* is not an artist, and he doesn't narrate the whole novel. In fact, Mortimer doesn't really narrate even a part of the novel; he is only a story-teller *in* it, and nothing more. But instead of an omniscient narrator who writes heavy and heavily ironic rhetoric like a cynical Jehovah, *Our Mutual Friend* has a narrator who is teasing and chameleon-like. Except for those two paragraphs of "my lords and gentlemen and honourable boards," the heavy rhetoric of *Our Mutual Friend* is given to the Veneerings' "fifth retainer" (p. 49) as an odd narrative joke. The omniscient narrator in *Bleak House* concludes his grand opening description of Chancery with the "warning," "Suffer any wrong that can be done you, rather than come here!" (p. 51); in *Our Mutual Friend,* the echo of this warning is given by the Veneerings' servant, "the Analytical Chemist," as he announces dinner: "Come down and be poisoned, ye unhappy children of men" (p. 51).

This change of roles—a "fifth retainer" borrowing the omniscient narrator's voice—begins to describe the difference between *Bleak House* and *Our Mutual Friend*, and to indicate the closer, more direct relation this later novel has to *David Copperfield.* Of course, the Analytical Chemist doesn't actually say "Come down and be poisoned" or either of his other strange lines—"Here is another wretched creature come to dinner; such is life" (p. 49) and "Chablis, sir?—You wouldn't if you knew what it's made of" (p. 52). These lines, like the Analytical's title, are the creation of the narrator's sense of humor. And humor, rather than heavy rhetoric, is the main characteristic of the narrator in *Our Mutual Friend*. He has an extremely wilful sense of humor, which calls attention to his character as narrator, making thus for a kind of reflexiveness in this novel not unlike that which earlier marked *David Copperfield*.

One of the things the narrative voice can do in works of fiction is require the major characters, the would-be heroes and heroines, to learn the values which the narrative voice professes. This is true, certainly, in much of the great English fiction from Jane Austen's novels through Joyce's *Ulysses*.

With the exception of novels like *David Copperfield* and *Great Expectations,* whose first person narrators tell their own stories, the development of a relationship between the central character and the narrator in terms of values is never more fully developed in Dickens's works than in *Our Mutual Friend.* But because of the narrator's odd manner it is difficult to get his values into focus, and more difficult still to reconcile those values with his manner. Further, though, Mortimer "might . . . be impressed" by the story he tells—his interest in it "is hidden with great pains, but it is in him" (p. 57)—he is "indolent," "unmoved" by everything (p. 55), and so "disconsolate" that he "won't talk" (p. 53); thus we scarcely expect him ever to find in himself anything like the energy or interest in the world that the narrator has. Mortimer hasn't despaired of the world, however, or of the possibility of doing something in it: "show me a good opportunity," he says, "show me something really worth being energetic about, and *I*'ll show you energy" (pp. 62–63). Meanwhile, "the only speck of interest" he has is in fantasizing about young Blight, his clerk: "Whether . . . he is always plotting wisdom, or plotting murder, whether he will grow up, after so much solitary brooding, to enlighten his fellow-creatures, or to poison them" (p. 62).

As Mortimer's attitude toward young Blight shows, he has a grim sense of humor that is seemingly alienated but still imaginative—and in this he is already somewhat like the narrator. But Mortimer isn't interested in the world, or at any rate is afraid to show his interest in it. The narrator's job, then, is to persuade Mortimer out of this retreat, and into active engagement with the world. The way he does this is to tease Mortimer's curiosity with the story of "the Man from Somewhere," otherwise known as the story of "Our Mutual Friend."

Henry James's novels almost always have a *ficelle*, a character whose role is to legitimize the bringing together of all the various pieces into a whole, the meaning of which James has decided to elucidate. James is the observer and the creator of meaning; the *ficelle* is his servant.[3] In *The Portrait of a Lady* Ralph Touchett is allowed to assume the role of creator, fabricating imaginatively the Isabelle Archer whom we so admire. But Ralph creates her for his own pleasure—and then he dies and leaves her. In *The Princess Casamassima* Hyacinth Robinson observes the world, lovingly, for James: his last tour of London is brilliant and beautifully moving as response to and understanding of the human situation. But then Hyacinth commits suicide. In most of the other James novels, creation and comprehension are reserved for the narrative voice. The meaning of the whole assemblage is unavailable to mere characters: the critical omniscience of "art" is required to make full sense of "life." The closest James comes to creating a character capable of "making a net of a number of . . . pieces" (DC, p. 70) is the *ficelle*, whose role, however, is not to understand but to assemble.

Dickens's novels rarely pay enough attention to plot realism—to legitimizing or justifying the bringing together of all the pieces—to want or need a *ficelle* figure,[4] though Mortimer may at first seem to be that kind of figure in *Our Mutual Friend* as he carries his story from one segment of the novel's world to another. But Mortimer's story is important, not for what it tells, but for its being Mortimer's story. In the midst of John Rokesmith's becoming "interested" in the story—it is, after all, about Rokesmith!—Dickens introduces a remark about Mortimer which says precisely that this is its importance: Rokesmith knows the story only "from Mrs. Boffin's accounts of what she heard from Mr. Lightwood, who seemed to have a reputation for his manner of relating a story, and to have made this story quite on his own" (p. 443). In the manuscript of *Our Mutual Friend*[5] this entire statement about Mortimer is added interlinearly (Ms. 200). It has nothing to do with the primary focus of the paragraph, and could conceivably have been omitted. Dickens writes it in, however, and in so doing tempts our interest away from Rokesmith and away from his interest in the story; instead we are invited to be interested in Mortimer. In the beginning, when Mortimer first tells the story, we are told that despite Society he could "be impressed by what he . . . relates" (p. 57); later, "to sustain his reputation," he expands the story to include its "sequel" (p. 470). In the end, though he tells Lady Tippins, "I mean to tell you nothing" (p. 888), he does provide the last installment of the story. Mortimer's story has become his gesture: and as such it tells us that he is an observer of the world.

For Dickens, observation is the most important human act. Observation—etymologically the act of guarding and saving more than simply watching—is itself already close to meaning because of its presumptive wholeness, for to know the world is to begin to save it. Thus the observing character as central character must come to know what Dickens knows: must learn the world of the novel. In a novel which has such an observer, the narrative voice and that character merge in the end, knowing and then valuing the same things; and we, as readers, are led along toward what they know and value.

Mortimer begins as a seemingly unimportant character, introduced at the Veneering dinner party after the Veneerings, the Podsnaps, Twemlow, Sophronia (disguised as the "mature young lady"), Alfred Lammle (ditto the "mature young gentleman"), and Lady Tippins. He is identified only as "a certain 'Mortimer,' another of Veneering's oldest friends" (pp. 52–53). Since Mortimer has "founded [himself] upon Eugene" (p. 337 and elsewhere), and Eugene professes to "know less about myself than about most people in the world" (p. 338), Mortimer would seem to be less than promising as a character. As the young people in the novel begin to pair—Eugene with Lizzie, John Harmon with Bella, Fledgeby with Georgiana, Sophronia with Lammle, Jenny *not* with Charley as her "Him" but eventually with Sloppy, Miss Peecher (in her own mind) with Bradley and Mary Anne thus with Charley, Mr. Venus with Pleasant Riderhood at last, and even George Sampson with Lavvy: as everybody gets more or less matched with somebody, Mortimer remains alone. The closest he comes to being paired is being claimed by Lady Tippins as one of her "lovers" (p. 54) and being suspected by Bella of wanting to propose to her (p. 519). In the end, he goes home to his rooms in the Temple alone.

But Mortimer is an important character in the novel: we can be sure of this from his being given the last scene. He is the last actor to leave the stage of *Our Mutual Friend*, and he leaves it triumphant. At the Veneerings' dinner party, Twemlow, following Mortimer's lead, asserts himself for once, and stands up against Society. As a result, "a canopy of wet blanket seems to descend upon the company." Watching, "Mortimer Lightwood alone brightens." And he doesn't just go home alone, then; he "fares to the Temple, gaily" (p. 892).

Gaiety is Dickens's new word for happiness, and it has to be taken seriously, just as happiness must. Things "radiant" and "shining," the "true golden gold" of hearts which turn "bright" and "sparkle" proliferate in the imagery Dickens uses to resolve *Our Mutual Friend*, and gaiety like Mortimer's is closely connected with such enlightenment. Gaiety is Mortimer's achievement at the end of the novel: he comes to it through what he has learned as a critical observer of the world and, to a lesser degree, through his new assertiveness in it.

Early in Book Four, the scene in which Bella tells John about her new "serious" attitude is interrupted by Pa Wilfer's coming to visit. Bella is "more than usually fantastic with him" (p. 751)—and we know by now that "fantastic" means something like "imaginatively serious." Bella asks Pa "how they have used [him] at school today," school being construed to mean both "the Mincing Lane establishment" where he works and Mrs. Wilfer's "Academy":

> "Why, to say the truth, both have taken a little out of me to-day, my dear, but that was to be expected. There's no royal road to learning; and what is life but learning!"
> "And what do you do with yourself when you have got your learning by heart, you silly child?"
> "Why then, my dear," said the cherub, after a little consideration, "I suppose I die."
> "You are a very bad boy," retorted Bella, "to talk about dismal things and be out of spirits."
> "My Bella," rejoined her father, "I am not out of spirits. I am as gay as a lark." (751–52)

What Pa defines in this brief dialogue with his daughter is tragedy. The achievement of tragedy comes with knowledge: once "you have got your learning by heart," Pa says—"after a little consideration"—you die. There is nothing left to do. The goal is the learning. If you understand the purpose of life the way Pa does—"what is life but learning!"—there is nothing "dismal" at all about death.

Pa "has no egotism in his pleasant nature" (p. 752), and

thus can't conceive of life in terms of possession. What you have—too little or too much, "poverty" or "wealth" (p. 376) —isn't what defines the "realities" of life; rather, what you know does. When knowledge is a good thing in Dickens's works, it is a comprehensive and understanding kind of knowledge which creates larger realities out of the fragments of life that we otherwise exist among. In its highest form it is called wisdom: and "Love . . . [is] the highest wisdom ever known upon this earth" (ED, p. 130).

Like most of Dickens's novels, *Our Mutual Friend* is often about learning. Lizzie has a "library of books" in the fire, "in the hollow down by the flare" (p. 73), and eventually gets Mr. Riah as her teacher. Charley goes to school "to be good, and get learning" (p. 118), and to "rise" in the world like Bradley has risen. Miss Peecher runs the girls' counterpart to Bradley's school, Miss Abbey runs the Six Jolly Fellowship-Porters like "a ready schoolmistress accustomed to bring her pupils to book" (p. 112), and Mrs. Wilfer pretends to keep a "Ladies' School" (p. 77). Betty Hidgen is proud that she can "read [her] Bible and most print" (p. 246); she keeps a "Minding-School" (p. 247). Sloppy, "a beautiful reader of a newspaper" on his own (p. 246), still stands "in need of some instruction" if he is to be helped to "an industrious and useful place in life" (p. 444); he is sent to school—with Bradley as his teacher— and at the end has "been a learning and a learning . . . ever so long" (p. 881). Old Mr. Harmon "wanted to know the nature and worth of everything that was found in the dust" (p. 129). Noddy Boffin suffers from having had his "Education neglected," and admires Wegg because "all Print is open to him" (p. 93); but Noddy knows that "there's some things . . . never found among the dust" (p. 136)—and that is an important bit of knowledge for Dickens. Mr. Podsnap, finally, leads the "school of Podsnappery" (p. 175); his personal motto is, perversely, "I don't want to know about it" (p. 174).

What is it important for us to know? Not facts, or amounts, or statistics, or what old Mr. Harmon would call the "nature and worth of everything" (p. 129): because, as Mortimer says to Mr. Boffin, "everything wears to rags" (p. 136). Mortimer is right: the things he means—things you can own or possess

—do indeed wear away to rags, to dust. When Noddy replies that "there's some things that I never found among the dust" he isn't contradicting Mortimer so much as redirecting his thought—to "some *things*" which aren't like "everything." In the manuscript, Noddy explains the point more fully than the printed text records. What he refers originally to are not "manufactured articles," but "articles not made, nor weighed, nor measured, nor bought, nor sold" (Ms. 71). What's "never found among the dust" is a different kind of reality, with a different—and higher—worth. It is like that "something—not an Ology at all" (HT, p. 225) that Mr. Gradgrind couldn't find, and like Daniel Doyce's wonderful invention—which "the Divine artificer had made . . . and he had happened to find" (LD, p. 570), and which Doyce can only describe as being "as true as it ever was" (LD, pp. 233, 569). Love doesn't wear to rags; wisdom and goodness and truth don't "wear out, as many things do" (p. 136). And Mr. Boffin would teach this humane lesson to the sceptical Mortimer.

Early in the novel John Rokesmith gets employment as Mr. Boffin's secretary, and busies himself learning how to assist the Golden Dustman. The narrator tells us that if in his earnestness Rokesmith "sought power, it was the power of knowledge, the power derivable from a perfect comprehension of his business" (p. 241). His "business" is a simple, straightforward one; but the definition of "power," so formulated, begs for generalization. In the context of so much learning and pursuit of learning, "the power of knowledge" is important. In becoming a "highly certificated stipendiary schoolmaster" (p. 265), Bradley has "acquired mechanically a great store of teacher's knowledge" (p. 266). But Bradley's knowledge is not "comprehension," even of his "business" as a teacher; his mind is only a "place of mechanical stowage," a "wholesale warehouse" (p. 266), and what he knows gives him no power at all. Similarly, Charley's "learning" doesn't make him "good," as Lizzie had hoped it would, because he has selfish ends in mind: his goal is "perfect respectability" (p. 781), not "perfect comprehension," and he figures to achieve that end "alone."

Eugene has to experience the usual Dickensian crisis of

adversity in order to reform. Mortimer, however, has few experiences of his own. He changes from that state of "lassitude and indifference, which had become his second nature" (p. 337), into a man of "infinite zest" who labors "with such unwonted despatch and intention, that a piece of work was vigorously pursued as soon as it was cut out" (p. 875), thanks to what he learns by observing the world. Because of what he comprehends, by means of reflection, he becomes "the voice of wisdom" (p. 885); and this is the voice that challenges, finally, the "voice of Society" (p. 889)—and wins. When Mortimer "sees Twemlow home, shakes hands with him cordially at parting, and fares to the Temple, gaily" (p. 892), he has achieved the end of the novel. He has finished his story, challenging Society with it, insisting boldly now on his values, and reserving his "indifference" (p. 889) for the false Society itself. He hears the "voice of Society" for what it is—cacophony—and responds, "gaily!"

To respond so to chaos takes faith: faith in "the power of knowledge," faith in what the imagination can teach and learn. At the end of *The Waste Land*—one of the original epigraphs for which was from *Our Mutual Friend*[6]—when this kind of faith is seemingly achieved and the fear of "death by water" overcome, "The boat responded/Gaily . . . your heart would have responded/Gaily."[7] In "Lapis Lazuli," Yeats writes out the full formula for our dealing with the madness of our world by means of what we know. At the end of their plays, he says, "Hamlet and Lear are gay;/Gaiety transfiguring all that dread." And the transfiguration, for Yeats, is none other than "Heaven blazing into the head:/Tragedy wrought to its uttermost."[8]

At the end of *Little Dorrit*, Amy and Arthur Clennam "went down" into the world, "into a modest life of usefulness and happiness":

> They went quietly down into the roaring streets, inseparable and blessed; and as they passed along in sunshine and shade, the noisy and the eager, and the arrogant and the froward and the vain, fretted and chafed, and made their usual uproar.
>
> (LD, 895)

Carried forward eight years, "the arrogant and the froward and the vain" are named Podsnap and Veneering and Lady

Tippins, and their noise is called "the voice of Society." At the end of *Little Dorrit*, the exciting thing, for us and for Dickens, is that Amy and Arthur can go down into that world, to live "happy and useful" lives. It is no longer necessary for Dickens to give his characters some sort of relief from the "uproar"; we are "in [the world] to be of it," and we "must mingle with it, and make the best of it, and make the best of [ourselves] into the bargain."[9] At the end of *Our Mutual Friend* the noise is just as loud—or it will be tomorrow, when Society gets over Twemlow's defection and recovers its "voice."

But the noise of Society is less a bother now, because Society has proved itself irrelevant to the larger, more significant life in which work can be done to "improve the world a little" (DC, p. 540). A new, active society—a wise and legitimate society, which values honesty and earnestness—is set up to challenge Podsnappery. As Noddy Boffin says, "it makes a pretty and promising picter" (p. 849). Bella turns out to be "true golden gold" (p. 844), and being thus "rich" will "have a great power of doing good to others" (p. 747). Married and established, the radiant young Harmons' "delightful occupation" in the world is "to set all matters right that had strayed in any way wrong" (p. 874), and Eugene and Mortimer, "in turning to at last . . . turn to in earnest" (p. 885). In *Little Dorrit*, Amy and Arthur descend into the world "quietly": much more surely and emphatically, Mortimer goes home in that same world "gaily."

The good people of the novel have learned a lot—and they have learned to identify what is real and valuable in the world: love, and truth, and learning itself. Podsnap and his tribe are exposed as false people who corrupt reality or retreat from it. Podsnap rejects the reality of people having "died in the streets, of starvation," because it "was not in good taste" (p. 187); he rejects the idea of Lizzie Hexam and her marriage to a "gentleman" (p. 889). Podsnap's grand gesture—"his right arm . . . clearing the world of its most difficult problems, by sweeping them behind him" (p. 174)—and his determination not to know are defeated in the novel by the analysis and articulation of what is real. The Chemist and Mr. Venus are nominally—symbolically—in charge of these operations, but

what is described under such headings is really a job shared
by Mortimer, as observer and story-teller, and the narrative
voice.

Mortimer isn't the only story-teller in *Our Mutual Friend*, of
course. As usual, Dickens's method of creating a focus is,
paradoxically, to involve everybody in it. We learn that Mortimer's importance in the novel is *as* a story-teller by noticing
that almost everybody tells stories. Wegg reads to Mr. Boffin,
Lizzie tells stories from what she sees "in the hollow down by
the flare" (p. 73)—that hollow, she says, is "the real world"
(p. 278)—and Jenny creates stories for herself, to ease her
pain. Bella's speech is full of references to fantastic stories,
and Sloppy has that wonderful dramatic ability to "do the
Police in different voices" (p. 246). Even Podsnap has an
inclination toward narrative: he tells himself the story, in full
but repetitive detail, of how "the world got up at eight, shaved
close at a quarter-past, breakfasted at nine, went to the City
at ten, came home at half-past five, and dined at seven" (p.
174).

But Mortimer's is the most significant story, the story of *Our
Mutual Friend*. And Mortimer is the significant story-teller. In
the end, he has learned what his novel tries to teach: that there
is no reason to be afraid of Society. Society—the Society that
parades itself dressed up as Podsnap and Veneering and Lady
Tippins—is a charade, a foolishness acted out, a pretense.
Mortimer has learned what the realities are, and Society isn't
among them. He begins the novel as an unwilling, "disconsolate" (p. 53) adjunct to Society, brought to the Veneerings'
against his will to tell his story. When prevailed upon to perform, he begins at once to mythologize the story, critically, so
that it carries both the facts which are available about John
Harmon and Mortimer's version of what those facts mean.
The story, then, is his vehicle; it carries his mild ironic protest
against Society and its values.

As Mortimer tells it, his story is terribly sentimental, hardly
the stuff for a nine hundred page novel. Old Harmon "chose
a husband" for his daughter, "entirely to his satisfaction." But
the daughter loved "that popular character whom the novelists call Another." Of course she remained true to Another,

and her "venerable parent—on a cold winter's night, it is said
—anathamatized and turned her out" (p. 56). Mortimer continues in this vein, reducing the story to cliche: "The pecuniary resources of Another were, as they usually are, of a very
limited nature . . . they lived in a humble dwelling, probably
possessing a porch ornamented with honeysuckle" (p. 56).
Mortimer's energy for this kind of parody wanes—"We must
now return, as the novelists say, and as we all wish they
wouldn't, to the man from Somewhere" (p. 57)—and his story
falters to a halt.

The sequel to this story, involving Bella and Eugene and
Lizzie, among others—Dickens's story—is more complex and
more interesting, for us as well as for Mortimer. The question
becomes the deep one of metaphysics rather than the surface
one of simple affection. The characters involved in these new
love stories have to establish themselves—as selves, individually—and learn or prove their own best worth before the
question of love can be resolved. Thus we watch Bella give up
the self which she describes to Lizzie as "shallow, cold,
worldly, limited"—"I am such a nasty little thing." she says
(p. 592)—and learn how to become instead a woman with "a
heart well worth winning . . . that once won, goes through fire
and water for the winner" (p. 592). The prospect of someday
achieving such a self turns Bella "serious" for the first time
(p. 593). Eugene finally becomes serious, too. He admits and
identifies himself, and begins then a new life. He becomes "a
true man" who—because he is such, at last—can follow "the
right course," and love and marry Lizzie. He can also quit
teasing Mortimer with his indifference: "Touch my face with
yours. . . . I love you, Mortimer" (p. 812). And Lizzie has to
change too. Though she is always good and loving, she
doesn't respect herself properly. She has to free herself from
the class prejudice that she so easily accepts, thinking of herself as "belonging to another station" (p. 761) and being "so
different" (p. 763) from Eugene. Then she can quit running
away from him.

John Harmon doesn't really change. He changes names, of
course, and in the end reclaims his identity as John Harmon,
but that is all symbolic rather than dramatic action. The story
of the man from Somewhere is supposedly the story of John

Harmon, and he is "Our Mutual Friend" (p. 157); but the
novel is not about him, really—and Mortimer only sees him
at the beginning, when he identifies himself as Julius Handford, and at the end, when he is forced to disclose his true
identity.

As Mortimer is drawn into following the stories of Bella,
Eugene, and Lizzie, he learns a new hope for humanity and
human society which changes him. Thus it is a new Mortimer
who returns to Society in the final chapter. He has "resolved"
to take another look at it (p. 886) in the previous chapter, and
therefore accepts an invitation to the Veneerings' for dinner:

> There is Lady Tippins. There are Podsnap the Great, and Mrs.
> Podsnap. There is Twemlow. There are Buffer, Boots, and
> Brewer. There is the Contractor, who is Providence to five hun-
> dred thousand men. There is the Chairman, travelling three
> thousand miles per week. There is the brilliant genius who
> turned the shares into that remarkably exact sum of three hun-
> dred and seventy five thousand pounds, no shillings, and no
> pence.
>   To whom, add Mortimer Lightwood, coming in among them
> with a reassumption of his old languid air, founded on Eugene,
> and belonging to the days when he told the story of the man from
> Somewhere. (887)

Mortimer's "reassumption of his old languid air" is of course
itself a disguise; he is now an "eminent solicitor" who works
with "despatch and intention" and "infinite zest" (p. 875).
When Mortimer first told his story, under duress, he warned
his audience that it wasn't "statistical" (p. 55), and thus
wouldn't interest them. When he returns to it in this last
chapter, the narrator introduces the element of statistical
identification in describing the Contractor, the Chairman,
and the "brilliant genius." Like "the Member, the Engineer,
the Payer-off of the National Debt, the poem on Shakespeare,
the Grievance, and the Public Office" at the Veneerings' first
party (p. 49), these characters are identified by what they do,
and their statistical embellishments are ironic extensions of
their metaphysically irrelevant occupational facts. In the con-
frontation that follows these introductions, our new Mortimer
argues against Society's attempt to classify us by what we do,
and in so doing argues—as the whole novel does—against the

idea of a class society. When Lady Tippins calls Lizzie "a female waterman" she is attempting to identify her the way Society identifies its own. Parodying Society, the narrator names its members as it would name them: Boots, Brewer, etc. (It is sheer narrative wickedness that reduces a left-over "Buffer, interposed between the rest of the company and possible accidents" at the first dinner party, to a character known as "Buffer.") Mortimer, however, rejects this method of identification and classification, and will no longer play Society's game, or even sit among them, alienated, refusing to talk. He is serious and "uncompromising" (p. 890) now in his resistance to Lady Tippins and Podsnap. Because of his seriousness, this last chapter—unlike earlier chapters at Veneering's or Podsnap's—is not satire. Mortimer is involved in the story now: he has really made it his own, and challenges Society with it. Lizzie is not "a female waterman," though "she sometimes rowed in a boat with her father." She is not "a factory girl," though "she had some employment in a paper mill" (p. 889). Mortimer is "amused" (p. 889) by the disturbance his challenge causes, and his mood "brightens" (p. 892) as Society's grows dull and the party fails.

When Mortimer "shakes hands with [Twemlow] cordially at parting, and fares to the Temple, gaily" (p. 892) he doesn't really go home alone, because the narrative voice is with him, sympathetically, appreciating his accomplishment. Mortimer has become a hero, for Dickens, by learning how to combine a serious critical knowledge of the world with a happy, energetic life in it.

That Dickens—or Dickens's narrator, at any rate: his artist-self—has managed to achieve this same combination in himself is evident in the attitude of the narrative voice throughout the novel. The narrator of *Our Mutual Friend* teases Society every time he writes of it, playing with it and laughing at it in his satire. But he indulges his sense of humor generally, involving almost every character and every kind of situation. Even the most serious moments are presented to us "gaily," created out of his knowledge of and happiness in the world.

Pa Wilfer is comically unafraid of death, because his simple understanding of life is tragic, and he can thus be "as gay as a lark" (p. 753). "Gaiety" works, as Yeats says, "transfiguring all that dread." When Bella first turns "serious," after her conversation with Lizzie, the narrator plays the most fanciful, fantastic trick of the whole novel in his representation of the world's response to "the brightness in [the] face" of this new Bella:

> O boofer Lady, fascinating boofer lady! If I were but legally executor of Johnny's will! If I had but the right to pay your legacy and to take your receipt!—something to this purpose surely mingled with the blast of the train as it cleared the stations, all knowingly shutting up their green eyes and opening their red ones when they prepared to let the boofer lady pass. (594)

The narrator transforms the world in a similar way when John and Bella marry—and the serious note consonant with the "bright old song" he sings there is the assertion that "there are days in this life, worth life and worth death" (p. 738).

When Mrs. Higden dies, the narrator is subdued and sober; he is tempted momentarily to "my lords and gentlemen and honourable boards" at her simple funeral, but resists the inclination to that rhetoric. Instead, he reports that "the Reverand Frank Milvey, comforting Sloppy, expounded to him how the best of us were more or less remiss in our turnings at our respective Mangles—some of us very much so—and how we were all a halting, failing, feeble, and inconstant crew" (p. 578). The brilliance of this consolation lies in the pun that resonates from mangling; in technique and in effect it is like David's quiet narrative reference to Jane Murdstone's nature in the scene following his mother's death.

Another face of the narrator's playfulness shows in his treatment of Silas Wegg. We know from his introduction— from the manner of his introduction—that he is going to be harmless in his lies and petty deceits, and that he thus belongs to the more simply comic part of the novel. But the narrator would extract serious meaning out of comedy as well as make tragedy gay. As Wegg reads to Mr. Boffin about misers, the narrator creates a wonderful meaning from the scene, going well beyond Wegg's own crude avarice. As this "literary man" reads, another literary man—the narrator—interrupts him with parenthetical reports of his actions which indicate

Wegg's involvement in the story he is reading and his application of it to his situation in Boffin's Bower. There is money
hidden everywhere in the story he is reading, and the more
he reads the more excited he gets: there must be money—old
Harmon's money—hidden in the Bower as well. As Wegg
entertains these thoughts, the narrator tells us, in paren-
theses, that his "wooden leg started forward under the table,
and slowly elevated itself as he read on" (p. 544). As the
"crisis" of discovering Daniel Dancer's hidden fortune approaches in the book, "Mr. Wegg's wooden leg . . . gradually
elevated itself more and more" (p. 544), until—at the climax
of the story—he suddenly "dropped over sideways" against
Mr. Venus "in a kind of pecuniary swoon" (p. 545). The
image is obvious enough—and funny enough! Its serious
meaning is that Wegg's lust for money is precisely that: lust.[10]

Our Mutual Friend is the funniest novel Dickens wrote,
though it is also one of the most serious. If ever there has
been a "mature" novel, this is it. If I pay close enough attention to the narrative voice as I read it, it seems almost like *The
Tempest*, in the lovely, serene richness of its comedy. The
narrator knows from the beginning what this world is, and
what it means. He writes the novel, then, as an act of
generosity, creating this world for its own pleasure and for
ours. For his own entertainment he mimics various of the
characters as he proceeds, adopting momentarily their manners, their styles. Sometimes, too, he lets the best of them
share his manner or style.

It is the narrator who renders Frank Milvey's lovely consolation to Sloppy as "how the best of us were more or less
remiss in our turnings at our respective Mangles"; but then
Frank himself says of Betty Higden's grave, as Sloppy lies
weeping on it, "Not a very poor grave . . . when it has that
homely figure on it. Richer, I think, than it could be made by
most of the monumental sculpture in Westminster Abbey" (p.
578). The rhetoric of this remark is Dickens's high rhetoric—
and it isn't usually shared with characters. That Frank Milvey
is allowed its use here indicates Dickens's serious respect for
him.

A comic example of this odd kind of sharing between narrator and character is Pa's participation in the narrator's joke

about Bella on the day she and John confess that they love
each other. John comes rushing in on Pa and Bella in Pa's
office and embraces her, so that she "seemed to shrink to next
to nothing in the clasp of his arms" (p. 671). After a few
moments Bella's "engaging tenderness" makes it "quite ex-
cusable in John Rokesmith to do what he did"—embrace her
again. But instead of telling us that John embraced her, the
narrator says, "What he did was, once more to give her the
appearance of vanishing as aforesaid" (p. 672). Soon John is
at it for a third time, "assisting Bella to another of those
mysterious disappearances" (p. 674). This time Pa is in on the
narrator's euphemistic joke, and says—"gaily, and not ex-
pressing disapproval"—"Well . . . when you—when you come
back from retirement, my love, and reappear on the surface,
I think it will be time to lock up and go" (p. 674).

The narrator of *Our Mutual Friend* is marvellously involved
in the dramatic life of the novel: there is probably no other
example of such narrative freedom in our literature before
Joyce's *Ulysses*. At the end, when Mortimer leaves the novel,
he and the narrator share fully a single understanding of its
world. This world is complex and difficult, and even dangerous: Eugene sees it as such, and plans to "fight . . . to the
last gasp" against Society, in order to make a worthy life for
himself and Lizzie (p. 885). But Mortimer has a larger understanding of the world than Eugene has. At the end Mortimer
doesn't feel threatened by Society, doesn't have to "fight" it.
He watches it, knows it, laughs at it. Like David, he leaves the
novel—ends it—happy. His story is complete now, and he
"fares to the Temple, gaily."

NOTES

1. Bradley's obsessive, diseased love and what it does to him are repeated
   and expanded in the character of John Jasper in *Edwin Drood.*
2. In recent criticism the most interesting and thought-provoking accounts of *Our Mutual Friend* are Edgar Johnson's in *Charles Dickens: His
   Tragedy and Triumph* (1952) and Garrett Stewart's in *Dickens and the Trials
   of the Imagination* (1974).
3. See M. Corona Sharp, *The Confidante in Henry James* (1963).
4. Madame Defarge with her knitting, of course, is the greatest *ficelle* of
   them all—but knitting is her gesture, not her role.
5. Manuscript in the Pierpont Morgan Library, New York.

6. "He do the Police in different voices"; see T. S. Eliot, *The Waste Land: A Facsimile and Transcript of the Original Drafts,* ed. Valerie Eliot (1971).
7. T. S. Eliot, *The Waste Land,* lines 418–21.
8. William Butler Yeats, "Lapis Lazuli," lines 16–20.
9. Dickens to Wilkie Collins, 6 September 1858.
10. Poor Wegg! Later in the same chapter "his self-willed leg" keeps thrusting itself into holes in the mounds, and jamming itself down into the ashes (p. 551).

CHAPTER 8

"Few Languages Can Be Read Until Their Alphabets Are Mastered."

The Mystery of Edwin Drood opens with an interior monologue. Dickens has written such before—in *Bleak House* for Tony Jobling's discovery of Krook's death, in *Our Mutual Friend* for Lizzie's right imagination of her father's death. This one is different, however, because it is the product of an opium dream. It is different, too, because it is the opening paragraph of the novel—and thus presents the reader with an almost impossible problem.

Dickens's novels always begin strikingly. In several he starts with reference to the setting he intends to establish. *Oliver Twist* opens with an odd and teasing reluctance, "in a certain town which for many reasons it will be prudent to refrain from mentioning . . . on a day and date which I need not take upon myself to repeat" (p. 45). *Barnaby Rudge,* in contrast, opens particularly: "In the year 1775 . . . at a distance of about twelve miles from London—measuring from the Standard in Cornhill" (p. 43). *Bleak House* and *A Tale of Two Cities* begin more mythically or symbolically, but they both begin in London. *Our Mutual Friend* opens the most particularly and realistically of all the novels, on the Thames, "between Southwark Bridge which is of iron, and London Bridge which is of stone" (p. 43), somewhere between 1819 and 1831. *Edwin Drood,* however, begins by questioning rather than describing the setting: "An ancient English Cathedral town? How can the ancient English Cathedral town be here!" (p. 37). It is the most striking—and the most difficult—opening of any of Dickens's novels.

These introductory questions are perhaps the key to the most important "mystery" of *Edwin Drood.* They are John

119

Jasper's questions, first of all: questions from his "scattered consciousness," about the reality of his world. They generalize, too: before we know that Jasper or anyone else in the novel exists, these questions are posed to us and for us. Thus we are taken into Jasper's extraordinary experience before we meet him or are told about him. He begins the novel then as "one of us"—to borrow Conrad's phrase—and not just as an evil man.

That we begin *Edwin Drood* with the representation of a mental reality is important, for it is primarily concerned throughout with mental states and psychological realities. At the end of this opening paragraph the initial mystery of this strange vision is solved. The ominous "spike of rusty iron" which contradicts "the real prospect" of Cloisterham turns out to be "the rusty spike on the top of a post of an old bedstead," and "the man whose scattered consciousness has thus fantastically pieced itself together" devotes a "vague period of drowsy laughter" to this solution (p. 37). But why should this character—he is as yet unnamed—have such a dream or vision? And why is he here, in an opium den?

When Scrooge awakens from his vision of the future in *A Christmas Carol,* the figure with whom he has been pleading has "dwindled ... into a bedpost" (CB I, p. 126)—but Scrooge believes the dream and is chastened by it, and changes himself and his way of life. Jasper, however, enjoys his strange dream, and undertakes it intentionally: it represents the future as he wills it. There is no question of ghosts here, or bits of "underdone potato" (CB I, p. 59); this dream is at once an indulged fantasy and a psychological reality. As a fantasy it is Jasper's dream of freedom from the "cramped monotony of [his] existence" (p. 48); as a psychological reality it represents the violence he is capable of committing to acquire what he wants to call his happiness. The "long procession" of soldiers and dancing girls and elephants and attendants toward the Sultan's palace are Jasper's dream translation of the clergy and choir of the Cathedral, I suppose; the dancing girls and the general exotic aspect of the scene suggest Rosa—but cannot name her, or even particularize an erotic desire; the spike is set up "maybe ... by the Sultan's orders for the impaling of a horde of Turkish robbers"—but more likely for Edwin Drood.

What is most remarkable about this opening dream is that someone is watching the details of it, trying to decipher them, trying to figure out both what they signify and how they match reality. The someone watching is—must be—both Jasper and you or me as reader. That Jasper must watch himself to find his meaning makes him at least in part a sympathetic character. That we too must look with "close scrutiny" (p. 156) at seemingly absurd and surreal details tells us at the outset how we must read this novel.

In chapter 2, when Tope the Verger says that Jasper "has been took a little poorly" during the vesper service, the Rev. Mr. Crisparkle is at first more concerned with the propriety of Tope's saying "took" to the Dean than with Jasper's illness, and the Dean is "not unflattered" by this attitude. It would be better, however, for both Crisparkle and the Dean to pay more attention to the substance of Tope's remark than to his manner—and better, too, for them to heed Jasper more than Jasper's manner.

We must watch every detail here. We must not be distracted, or let ourselves be misled. If we read as Dickens would have us read, we will find the focus clear and unremittingly singular. This is his last "net"—and it's an exemplary one, a marvelous and fantastic net that catches everything and makes it show its meaning.

There are more than enough analyses of Jasper's character in print; I won't try my hand at another. Instead, I wish to focus on the roles of two other characters, Hiram Grewgious and Dick Datchery, and on the way in which the narrative voice conducts the novel. I hope to demonstrate through this analysis the relation of *Edwin Drood* to *David Copperfield* and to *Our Mutual Friend;* and I hope to convince you, in the end, that *Edwin Drood* is Dickens's last complete—and completed— novel.

We have to begin with Jasper and his dream, however, because of what it means to begin the novel inside Jasper's drugged head. *Edwin Drood* is a strange and difficult novel partly because its focus is so much on the negative side of

things. Jasper and his twisted, perverse affection for Rosa Bud
and Edwin occupy most of our attention; Crisparkle, who is
good and innocent and knows that true "Love" is "wisdom"
(p. 130), is a minor character as well as a Minor Canon. *Edwin
Drood* is a study of evil as a disease, a pathological examination more detailed and explicit than any Dickens had ever
written.[1] He had always had the eye of the diagnostician, as
modern medical literature has so profusely illustrated; but he
was also guilty, as late as *David Copperfield,* of a sentimental
matching of physical and moral characteristics. In *Edwin Drood*
Dickens creates Jasper as an individual, however, not a
stereotype: and he makes the particular connections among
his physical, mental, and moral states utterly convincing. We
can understand his evil as a disease, and we can see the disease destroying him. We have access to what goes on in his
mind—in its opiated state of freedom—and know that he
indulges himself in his evil. The various characters in the
novel who observe Jasper have no such privileged access, but
must learn what he is by observing how he acts. What they
learn matches our more familiar knowledge of him; and at the
end the most important characters—Grewgious, Rosa's faithful guardian, and Dick Datchery, whose only role in the novel
is Jasper-watching—seem confident in their knowledge of
him, that in his evil he will destroy himself.

David's need to know evil—to understand and comprehend
it, along with everything else—seemed but a minor theme in
his novel, and only occasionally demanded either David's attention or ours. Here, however, we must deal with evil—learn
it, and learn how to deal with it—before we can enjoy the
pleasures of society and civilization. Jasper's evil is oppres-
sive, and like most evil it is pervasive in its influence. It in-
vades the very atmosphere, and affects everyone—including
you and me, I suspect. The only "person" free from this
oppression is the narrator, who is so far from being oppressed
or depressed or repressed—by Jasper's being "*ad*verse or *per*-
verse, or the *re*verse" (p. 210)—that he laughs and jokes
about almost everything. He can do so only because he knows
everything: and such a state is what he, like David before him
in his quieter way, invites us to.

This is another novel about looking at the world we live in and the need to know that world. As we might expect, there are a number of characters in the novel who watch and observe, and a number of references to knowing and needing to know. There are also numerous warnings given, and a variety of guardians—watchers also, etymologically—assigned to the young people who inhabit the world.

Warnings are given by several characters, in more or less serious seeming ways. Jasper gives Edwin "a warning" of what his true self is (p. 49); but his nephew, in his innocence—in his boyish blindness to any other than his own view of the world—"won't be warned" and "can't be warned" (p. 50). Jasper also warns Grewgious, curiously, of some danger ahead for Edwin and Rosa:

> "God bless them both!" [said Grewgious.]
> "God save them both!" cried Jasper.
> "I said, bless them," remarked the former, looking back over his shoulder.
> "I said, save them," returned the latter. "Is there any difference?" (119)

The Princess Puffer warns Edwin, too, that his is "a bad name to have just now": "A threatened name. A dangerous name" (p. 179). On the comic side, Deputy delivers his "warning" cry to Durdles throughout the novel (pp. 72, 76, 159); his only appearance bereft of that lovely song is in the end, when he acts as Datchery's ally. Early on, as Jasper clinks the keys to three of the Cathedral's tombs together, Durdles tells him, "Take care of the wards" (p. 70)—the "wards" being the cuts and notches in the keys. Except for the pun, the warning here is seemingly meaningless and irrelevant, unless its purpose is to draw attention to Jasper's musing interest in tombs and keys to tombs. Later, when Jasper joins Durdles on their allegedly "unaccountable sort of expedition" to the Cathedral (p. 151), Durdles warns him again: " 'Ware that there mound"—which turns out to be "quick-lime": "quick enough to eat your boots . . . quick enough to eat your bones" (p. 152).

If we read the novel thinking of a "mystery" and trying to solve a crime, this last warning will lead us to suspect that

Jasper buries Edwin's body in quick-lime, to dispose of it. If, however, we read the novel like a Dickens novel—and Dickens has never really written mysteries—this line will mean something very different. If we read *Edwin Drood* as a pathological examination of passion, we will read Durdles's warning as literally a warning to Jasper, and an ironically meaningful signal to us. Jasper is a man who is being eaten up from within by his own evil, who at the climactic moment will disintegrate before our eyes into "a heap of torn and miry clothes upon the floor" (p. 192).

The focus of warning always comes back to Jasper. We are told in the middle of chapter 12 that there is a "lamp" in his window at the Gate House, which "burns red behind his curtain, as if the building were a Lighthouse" (p. 154). This detail, however, is placed in the chapter artificially. The paragraph in which it is introduced describes Jasper and Durdles "descending into the crypt" of the Cathedral, and the following paragraph begins with their "locking themselves in . . . the crypt" (p. 154). We are around the corner from Jasper's house, intending into the crypt with them when the narrator suddenly and without apparent reason steps back to look at Jasper's window with its light burning in it. He takes us out of our way, quite literally, to make us see Jasper's light. The next time we see Jasper's "red light" is on the evening of the last meeting of Edwin and Neville Landless, on Christmas Eve; it "burns steadily all the evening in the lighthouse" (p. 182). On both occasions the light is obviously meant to forebode evil: a lighthouse, after all gives a warning to anyone "on the tide of busy life" to avoid that place. But the symbol isn't justified—legitimized in the narrative fabric of the novel— unless we see the focus for all warnings, narrative or otherwise, as upon Jasper. Near the end of the novel we come back to the image, and this time the narrator justifies it in relation to what a character is doing:

> John Jasper's light is kindled, and his Lighthouse is shining when Mr. Datchery returns alone towards it. As mariners on a dangerous voyage . . . may look along the beams of the warning light . . . so Mr. Datchery's wistful gaze is directed to this beacon, and beyond. (276)

The Lighthouse warns us, legitimately now, to beware of Jasper: the narrator was right all along in his seemingly peculiar and melodramatic description of Jasper's Gate House.

Just before the first reference to the Lighthouse there is a related narrative trick involving lights and the focus on Jasper. Durdles, the Dean, Tope, and Jasper part company: Durdles allegedly "going home to clean [him] self." Then follows an elaborate digression, seemingly, on the Cloisterham lamplighter, before we are told what the Dean, Tope, and Jasper do:

> The lamplighter now dotting the quiet Close with specks of light, and running at a great rate up and down his little ladder with that object—his little ladder under the sacred shadow of whose inconvenience generations had grown up, and which all Cloisterham would have stood aghast at the idea of abolishing—the Dean withdraws to his dinner, Mr. Tope to his tea, and Mr. Jasper to his piano. There, with no light but that of the fire, he sits chanting choir-music in a low and beautiful voice, for two or three hours; in short, until it has been for some time dark, and the moon is about to rise.

The digression about the lamplighter and his ladder pretends to hide the main clause of the sentence, which sends the Dean "to his dinner," Tope "to his tea," and Jasper *not* to eat, but to sit musing at "his piano." What the lamplighter really illuminates, of course, is Jasper's strange preoccupation; and his lamp is amplified by the "light . . . of the fire."[2] Watching is very closely associated with warning as a motif. The most significant action of the novel is watching. No matter what goes on in a scene—no matter what its simple action is—there is another dimension in which that action is complicated by a separate act of watching.[3] The first paragraph of the first chapter gives us details of Jasper's opium dream; more important than the details, however, is the form in which they are presented, as the question of an observing dreamer. When he awakens—his "scattered consciousness [having] thus fantastically pieced itself together"—he "looks around." The Princess Puffer speaks to him, and again "He looks about him" (p. 37). He "looks with repugnance at his three companions," and "notices" the woman herself. "What visions can *she* have?" he "muses . . . looking down" at her (p.

38). He "watches"; the "watcher" makes "a watchful pause," and then departs "with some reassured nodding of his head" (p. 39) to indicate that he understands—something.

The second chapter opens with a remark about our having "observed" the metaphorically clerical rook; we then are led to watch one such bird—Jasper—watching his nephew. He "looks on intently," with "a look of intentness and intensity —a look of hungry, exacting, watchful, and yet devoted affection." That look "is always, now and ever afterwards, on the Jasper face whenever the Jasper face is addressed in Edwin's direction" (p. 44). And while Jasper watches Edwin, the narrator watches Jasper, from a very carefully created distance. "Fixed as the look the young fellow meets is," he tells us, "there is yet in it some strange power of suddenly including the sketch over the chimneypiece" (p. 44). At the narrator's direction, we are dissociated from Jasper, looking at his face as it watches Edwin; suddenly we realise that it is also looking over our shoulder, as it were, at Rosa's picture as well.

A few moments later we watch Jasper drink a toast to Rosa, at Edwin's invitation:

> Laying an affectionate and laughing touch on the boy's extended hand, as if it were at once his giddy head and his light heart, Mr. Jasper drinks the toast in silence. (45)

The sentence is a trick: the "affectionate and laughing touch" of the dependent clause is squelched by the main clause, when we finally reach it at the end of the sentence. The rhetorical form and the rhythm of the sentence both contribute to this reversal, the effect of which is to make us see Jasper's act as double.

After the toast, Edwin proposes that he and Jasper "have a little talk." The prop Dickens offers them to accompany their conversation is "two pairs of nut-crackers." Once these are introduced, the narrative voice limits his commentary to notice that Jasper's "concentrated face again includes the portrait" of Rosa, and that Edwin, "glancing up at the sketch with complacency, and then shutting one eye ... [takes] a corrected prospect of it over a level bridge of nut-cracker." Otherwise, the only interruption of their dialogue is the repeated noise of their cracking walnuts: "Crack . . . Crack. On

Mr. Jasper's part . . . Crack. On Edwin Drood's part. Crack. On Mr. Jasper's part." The scene ends with three short one-line paragraphs:

Crack. Crack. Crack. Slowly, on Mr. Jasper's part.
Crack. Sharply, on the part of Edwin Drood.
Silence on both sides. (46)

"Crack" is a narrative statement, a direction. It says *pay close attention: watch.*

And as we watch, suddenly Jasper's face changes. "Good Heaven, Jack," Edwin says; "you look frightfully ill!" Jasper explains the sudden change as the result of his "taking opium for a pain"—and then admits that it is not just a physical pain, like rheumatism: "I have been taking opium for a pain—an agony," he says. Then he tells Edwin, "Look away from me." Edwin does so, "scared . . . casting his eyes downward." The narrator, however, lets us watch Jasper as he "recovers" himself. Then, "When Jasper is restored, he lays a tender hand upon his nephew's shoulder, and [speaks] in a tone of voice less troubled than the purport of his words—indeed with something of raillery or banter in it." The second half of this sentence is our reward for watching closely. The "purport of [the] words" that Jasper utters is ominous in a general way and ironic, perhaps, in a more particular sense: "There is said to be a hidden skeleton in every house" (p. 47). But most important is the narrative direction which describes the difference between Edwin's innocent understanding of his uncle and the narrator's. The difference between Jasper's "tone of voice" and "the purport of his words" is our clue. "Crack. Crack. Crack." Listen carefully: and *this* is what you should hear!

This scene of watching and listening develops into Jasper's explanation of his self-repression and unhappiness, which in turn is the source of his "warning" Edwin, and insisting that he "know" his uncle's situation. That these three activities—watching, knowing, and warning—come together here prepares us for their similar purposeful conflations elsewhere in the novel. As these critical acts are brought together, they are brought so for our benefit: because more so than in any other novel—of Dickens's or anybody else's, I suspect—*Edwin Drood* is written for our edification, for our entertainment.

"Entertain" is an interesting word. It is one of that large number of words in our language—borrowed, put together out of other languages—that suggest how naturally social we are, and what our social obligations are. "To entertain" means, etymologically, "to hold (oneself) among": to hold oneself among the things one sees, to become the creative and intelligent center of them, to make a world. Thus we can't be entertained; there is no place for or possibility of passive entertainment in this world. Again, we "are in it, to be of it." As Havelock Ellis said, talking of the role of the audience or viewer of a work of art, "Prospero is the Ideal Spectator of the Theatre."[4]

In the previous chapter I called *Our Mutual Friend* a "mature" novel. Now I want to call *Edwin Drood* a "last" novel— and suggest that in its lastness it is not unlike *The Tempest,* perhaps, though its manner may make it seem so. Before the word "world" can mean "what a man sees" or "a man's life" it means something more simple, etymologically, like "man's age" or even "old man." [5] You only have a world as an old man: the world is what you see, in your life. A world comes to you only at the end—and presumably at the full end—of life. I suppose that that is why the ancient Greeks argued that you couldn't call anyone happy until he or she had reached the end of life. At the very last you get your world, your everything; and then, letting that go, you get the universe— which is *really* everything—and you die.

The narrator of *Edwin Drood* works throughout the novel to bring together for us both the pieces of his world and his ways of making them his world. *Edwin Drood* offers us the chance to practice that kind of critical observation that has been Dickens's special talent all along—and it keeps reminding us how to make that observation, too, reiterating in subtle ways the steps of the critical process. In chapter 6, for example, nothing happens as far as the progress of the novel is concerned. Deputy is introduced: that's all. But at the end of this short episode, Durdles asserts that he "comes by *his* knowledge through grubbing deep for it" (p. 76), and Deputy cries

"Warning!" (pp.76, 77), and Jasper—opium pipe in hand, prepared for the dreams he so enjoys—"stands looking down upon [Edwin] . . . with a fixed and deep attention" (p. 77). Durdles knows, Deputy warns, Jasper watches: the three are unconnected, discrete. But we put them together in our reading. We take warning and watch, and from watching we come to know: that as Jasper looks down upon his nephew, he is thinking of that nephew buried deep under the Cathedral— or more precisely for this fantastic moment, that as he looks down upon him he is setting his nephew's image for the dream he so enjoys, and that in his dream Edwin will appear impaled on that "grim spike" we saw in the beginning atop the Cathedral. Edwin "lies asleep, calm and untroubled" as his uncle looks at him, "lights his pipe, and delivers himself to the Spectres it invokes at midnight" (p. 77). Edwin's sleep should not be so "calm and untroubled"; in the world his uncle inhabits—the world of "Spectres . . . at midnight"—he is already in danger.

Jasper also watches Rosa. In the terrible scene in which he so frightens her, his attention to her is seemingly excused even before it is represented: "It was a consequence of his playing the accompanyment without notes, and of her being a heedless little creature very apt to go wrong, that he followed her lips most attentively, with his eyes as well as hands; carefully and softly hinting the key-note from time to time." To play "without notes," however, is eerily paradoxical—if we take "notes" to be notes on the piano as well as a score to play from. And such a reading is legitimate: the narrator tells us that his "hinting the key-note . . . ever and again" sounds "as though it were a low whisper from himself" (p. 92) and not a sound made by the piano at all. Jasper's accompanyment, thus, is perverse; the excuse given for his watching her is a false one. It is doubly false, in fact, since Rosa isn't such a "heedless little creature," either. Though she doesn't look at Jasper as she sings, she is desperately aware of his watching her, and of the perverse way in which he is watching her.[6]

To help us focus our attention on the act of looking—on the fact of Jasper's indulgence in his desires for Rosa—the paragraph which introduces this scene details every one's "looking." Jasper follows Rosa "with his eyes"; Helena stands next to her, "with a face far more intent on Mr. Jasper than on [Rosa's] singing." Helena and Neville exchange a glance of special "recognition," and "Mr. Crisparkle saw, or thought he saw," their understanding of each other in that glance. Neville then leans against the piano, "admiring" Rosa. Edwin alone looks at nothing; in his innocence or carelessness, he plays distractedly with Miss Twinkleton's fan. And Miss Twinkleton herself rounds out the focus, assuming the "sort of exhibitor's proprietorship in the accomplishment on view, which Mr. Tope, the Verger, daily claimed in the Cathedral service" (p. 92).

This last sentence not only underlines Rosa's being "on view," it connects this scene to the scenes in the Cathedral—at the beginning, in the middle, and again at the end—in which Jasper is "on view." Its doing so reminds us that it is much more important here, in this instance, to watch Jasper watching than it is to watch Rosa and what happens to her. The reference to Tope and the scenes of "the Cathedral service" is on the surface apposite to Miss Twinkleton's situation here; what the introduction of Tope and the Cathedral actually does, however, is establish the place of this paragraph in the plan of the whole novel. It enlarges the context of the scene and at the same time particularizes its focus—on Jasper.

Jasper watches Rosa twice more: when she and Edwin go out for a walk (p. 170), and when he accosts her with his "love" for her in the garden at the Nuns' House (pp. 225–31). The first of these contrasts the new kind of love—friendship —that Edwin and Rosa now have for each other with Jasper's passion. The second occurs in a scene much like the one discussed above—so much so that the narrator connects it with "that night at the piano" (p. 227).

When Jasper asks at the Nuns' House to "see" Rosa (p. 225), she decides to come to him in the garden because so many of the school's "windows" look out upon it, and she "can be seen" there (p. 226). As the scene begins, we look first at Rosa: "she has never seen him since the fatal night," and from "the moment she sees him" now "she cannot look up at him for abhorrence." Then we look at Jasper, for the most part from her perspective: and what she senses most is the way he looks at her. "His eyes are . . . fixed upon her," and "she knows he is closely watching" her (p. 226); she is "conscious of his looking at her with a gloating admiration" (p. 227). When she tries to leave him, "his face looks so wicked . . . that her flight is arrested by horror as she looks at him"; "Looking at him," with "his face, darkly threatening" (p. 228), she cannot leave. He knows that he is being watched, that "many windows command a view" of them; and because he is being watched he becomes a "lie." There is an extreme "contrast between the violence of his look and delivery, and the composure of his assured attitude" (p. 228), "his easy attitude rendering his working features . . . absolutely diabolical" (p. 229). Our seeing him in this way is a privilege: "his talk would seem from the windows . . . to be of the airiest and playfullest" (p. 230), and as he leaves her he "goes away with no greater show of agitation than is visible in the effigy of Mr. Sapsea's father" (p. 231). When Rosa faints upon entering the house, Miss Twinkleton's maids misunderstand; they think it is "the hot and stifling air" that has overcome her (p. 231). But we understand what we have seen—and though Rosa "looks . . . as though she were trying to piece together" what has been presented to her "only in fragments" (p. 230), we comprehend the meaning of what we see in watching Jasper.

One of the most serious general warnings given in *Edwin Drood* is about how we look at things. The world is full of untruth, falseness, and disguise, and requires of us "close scrutiny" (p. 156). Gestures like Deputy's habitual response —"Yer lie!"—and the Billickin's determination against underhandedness, deceit, and disguise function to remind us regularly of what the narrator finally says outright: "seeming may be false or true" (p. 272). Those who watch Jasper must learn the difference between the two, and must learn it as a metaphysical lesson, again, not a moral one. The model of goodness is Crisparkle—who is always something more substantial than simply good. He is one of "the truest of men" (p. 196), a "true soul" (p. 206) with a "wholesome mind" (p. 124) and a healthy body; his "mind and body [are] as clear as crystal" (p. 181), and there is nothing of "false pretense" in his "nature" (p. 264). On the other side from this "true" character are three false men, two of whom are useful mainly in helping us to see the third. Luke Honeythunder is a parody of philanthropy when he first appears, and then—as Crisparkle proves in dismissing him—a charade of charity and honor. He is a mockery of all morality, genuine only in being a genuinely false man. Likewise Thomas Sapsea, "the purest Jackass in Cloisterham" (p. 62), is pure only in his stupidity: in his proud mockery of the Dean he too is a false man, a man who in his vanity sets himself and his "knowledge of the world" (p. 66) against all reality.

The third false man is Jasper. Like Honeythunder and Sapsea, he hides himself behind a façade of presumptive morality. As Choir Master of the Cathedral he is a minor canon, presumably, though perhaps he has not in fact taken orders, as Edwin thinks he is a "Lay Precentor, or Lay Clerk" (p. 48). Everyone assumes that he has "found [his] niche in life" and loves both to teach and to sing; but his true response to the "cramped monotony" of his vocation is "hate" (pp. 48–49). Knowing, then, what he thinks of his music—"It often sounds to me quite devilish," he says (p. 48)—we must beware when he sings so perfectly as he does on Christmas Eve. He is "in beautiful voice this day," and sings "the pathetic supplication to have his heart inclined to keep this law. . . . with such skill and harmony" that "he quite astonishes his fellows by his melodious power." He has achieved this perfection "probably . . . through a grand composure of the spirits" (p. 180): and "probably" as a narrative qualification suggests not that his success may come from some other source but that we must suspect his composure and the elements of his composition. When he speaks to Crisparkle about "having been out of sorts" but being "in a healthier state now," he draws a comparison between the two of them—"You had but little reason to hope that I should become more like yourself"—and reminds us that health, particularly metaphysical health, is a matter of both "mind and body" (p. 181). As they part, Jasper "sings, in a low voice," and "it still seems as if a false note were not within his power to-night" (p. 182). But he is not like Crisparkle, "mind and body, as clear as crystal": momentarily

Jasper's "face is knitted and stern," then "it clears immediately"—and we know from this change that his "composure"
is false. Music, for Jasper, is "an Art which [brings] him into
mechanical harmony with others"—but "the spirit of the man
[is] in moral accordance or interchange with nothing around
him" (p. 264).

As watching Jasper is what *Edwin Drood* is about, learning
to discriminate between "false" and "true" becomes one of
its central themes. The most important Jasper observers are
Grewgious and Dick Datchery, though in the end almost everyone seems to be watching him. Throughout the novel various characters observe him or each other, and their
observations reinforce, collectively, the general focus on
"close scrutiny" which the novel recommends to us if we are
to know what we must about this world.

Miss Twinkleton introduces this larger motif of watching in
the third chapter, as she and Mrs. Tisher make their regular
raids on the parlor at the Nuns' House during Edwin's visit
there, "affecting to look for some desiderated article" (p. 55).
Everyone in this novel has to watch or be watched, it seems,
from Deputy on the look-out for Durdles and lies to Datchery
on the look-out for Jasper—and the truth.

Crisparkle has to look carefully at Tartar—he "concentrated his attention on [his] handsome face" (p. 243)—before
he can recognize or remember him. Then Grewgious has an
idea, involving Tartar, of how to avoid any "watchman"
whom Jasper may have "set to watch" for Neville (p. 245).
Earlier, Grewgious entertains "a sort of fancy of having [Nev-
ille] under [his] eye" (p. 212). Grewgious doesn't usually have
fancies; he claims that he has no "imagination" every chance
he gets. But he is an observant man, and he comprehends the
meaning of what he observes.

The most important scene in the novel is that in which
Grewgious explains to Jasper that Edwin and Rosa parted on
Christmas Eve planning not to be married, and then observes
the fit that comes upon him. As Grewgious prepares to tell
Jasper of Edwin's and Rosa's resolution, he "move[s] his eyes
from the fire to his companion's face," again "look[s] at the
fire" (p. 190), and then keeps "his eyes on the fire." Once he

actually begins his recital, Grewgious watches Jasper's face with unbroken attention, "looking fixedly at him sideways, and never changing . . . his look in all that follow[s]" (p. 191). In six brief sentences, Grewgious tells Jasper all he has to tell him. The narrator, however, punctuates these sentences with four formulaic repetitions of Grewgious watching Jasper, and the scene extends dramatically: "Mr. Grewgious saw a staring white face. . . . Mr. Grewgious saw a lead-colored face. . . . Mr. Grewgious saw a ghastly figure rise. . . . Mr. Grewgious saw the ghastly figure throw back its head, clutch its hair with its hands, and turn with a writhing action from him" (p. 191). He concludes, then: "I have now said all I have to say"—

> Mr. Grewgious heard a terrible shriek, and saw no ghastly figure, sitting or standing; saw nothing but a heap of torn and miry clothes upon the floor.
> Not changing his action even then, he opened and shut the palms of his hands as he warmed them, and looked down at it. (192)

What Grewgious watches is Jasper's disintegration, his spontaneous combustion, the fit of mental anguish that consumes his form, the psychological cancer that devours his bones. This is the evidence of poor Jasper's metaphysical evil. Rosa later harbors a "suspicion" of Jasper in her "imagination" (pp. 232, 265); thanks to what he has observed in this scene, Grewgious knows Jasper's evil in his imagination, though to Rosa "he [makes] no mention of a certain evening when he warmed his hands at the Gate House fire, and looked steadily down upon a certain heap of torn and miry clothes upon the floor" (p. 265).

Earlier, when Jasper and Durdles set out to the Cathedral for their evening's exploration together, Jasper sees Crisparkle and Neville. Stopping behind a wall to keep from being seen, Jasper "watches . . . watches Neville as though his eye were at the trigger of a loaded rifle" (p. 152). Dickens is not ignorant of the proper use or handling of a rifle, or of its nomenclature. He means—we have learned to trust him, surely, by now—that Jasper looks at Neville "as though his eye were at the trigger of a loaded rifle." To place your eye at the sight is to aim; but to place your eye at the trigger is to shoot with your eye; to commit the act, wishfully, with the eye. The crime here is Jasper's *inside* crime, again: the crime is in the watching.

Durdles has begun casually "munching some fragments from his bundle" as soon as they stop. As he sees the "sense of destructive power . . . expressed in [Jasper's] face . . . Durdles pauses in his munching, and looks at him, with an unmunched something in his cheek" (p. 152). When Crisparkle and Neville leave,

> Mr. Jasper moves. But then he turns to Durdles, and bursts into a fit of laughter. Durdles, who still has that suspended something in his cheek, and who sees nothing to laugh at, stares at him until Mr. Jasper lays his face down on his arms to have his laugh out. Then Durdles bolts the something, as if desperately resigning himself to indigestion. (153)

The small detail of that "unmunched something" is curiously important. Repeated, it calls an odd attention to itself. We have no way of understanding what it means until we get to the end of the scene between Grewgious and Jasper, three chapters later. When Jasper recovers from the fit which leaves him but "a heap of torn and miry clothes upon the floor," Mrs. Tope arrives and urges him to eat. Ordinarily, Grewgious thinks first of food in any situation. This time, however, when Jasper asks him to "take something" with him, Grewgious replies, "I couldn't get a morsel down my throat, I thank you" (p. 193). Like Durdles, Grewgious is certain that what he has just seen will cause him indigestion. Like Durdles, he has just seen Jasper's guilt, his terrible evil; and as Durdles "sees nothing to laugh at" (p. 153) with Jasper, so Grewgious sees no reason—no possibility— for being social or sociable with him.

The other major Jasper watcher is Dick Datchery. Like the Princess Puffer, he comes to Cloisterham for the purpose of watching Jasper. The Princess first comes "looking for a needle in a haystack" (p. 178); she wants to learn Jasper's "secret," and is "unwinking, catlike, and intent" as she "observes" him (pp. 270–272). Following him, she "watches" and "peeps," "sees" him; "watching" and "comprehending" his intention, she "holds him in view" (p. 272). She loses him

momentarily in Cloisterham, but is aided by a gentleman—
Datchery—who sits in a window, "eyeing all who pass."
Datchery asks her, "Who are you looking for?" (p. 273), and
tells her that she may "see" Jasper at the Cathedral every day.
The next morning, after the service, Datchery accosts her:

> "Well, mistress. Good morning. You have seen him?"
> "*I*'ve seen him, deary. *I*'ve seen him."
> "And you know him?"
> "Know him! Better far, than all the Reverend Parsons put
> together know him."

The Princess's response satisfies Datchery. He has gone to the
service expressly to watch her watch Jasper. Deputy—re-
named "Winks" (p. 276) by Datchery, because he watches—
also goes to the Cathedral to watch her watch Jasper. He
"peeps, sharp-eyed," and "stares astounded" at what he sees
(p. 279). But Datchery is satisfied, not astounded, both with
what he sees and with what the Princess says to him.

When the Princess tells Datchery her story of having met
Edwin, he feels "justified in scoring up" nothing more than
"a moderate stroke" upon the cupboard door where he keeps
his secret tally "against" Jasper (p. 278). Settling down to his
breakfast after speaking with the Princess this second time, he
"adds one thick line to the score, extending from the top of
the cupboard-door to the bottom; and then falls to with an
appetite" (p. 280). We are not told what Datchery's strange
"scoring" means—but we know, nonetheless, that it is a
recording of Jasper's evil. We are not told why the Princess
is so triumphant at having seen Jasper in his role as Choir
Master in the Cathedral—but again we know. She has watched
him prove himself a false man, a wicked man. And to know
that, securely, is a substantial achievement, a triumph.

Knowing is always a substantial achievement, for Dickens.
If anything can save us in this world, knowing can. But it's
hard work. Dickens insists that knowledge is not a "gift," but
something that must be "worked out" (p. 76). "Durdles
comes by *his* knowledge through grubbing deep for it," and
that's the kind of work that Dickens recommends for us. Crisparkle urges Neville on in his studies by arguing the value of
knowledge, and advising him to "expect no miracle to help
[him]" (p. 209). The truth, he tells Neville, will "right" him;

and Neville answers, "So I believe, and I hope I may live to know it" (P. 209).

Edwin Drood is full of knowing and learning, of schools and references back to former school-days. It emphasizes understanding and wisdom, and it does so partly by showing us misunderstanding and stupidity. Sapsea is the chief witness for the latter. He is introduced as "the purest Jackass in Cloisterham" (p. 62); later he is a "solemn idiot" (p. 149) who speaks a "maze of nonsense" (p. 188). He is false both in his imitation of the Dean and in his pretense to knowledge and wisdom. Dickens doesn't worry much about his "dressing at" the Dean; people are always pretending to morality and piety, and Sapsea's "intoning in his pulpit" at sales and "bestowing a benediction on the assembled brokers" is no more sacrilegious than what goes on in the Cathedral. But Sapsea compounds his vanity by mimicking wisdom, and for this Dickens makes him and his foolishness seriously guilty by association. Dickens allows Jasper to use Sapsea, and then makes this connection reflect on Jasper. Sapsea's ignorance and colossal egotism match Jasper's hypocritical manipulation of the truth and his wicked self-indulgence. Jasper panders to Sapsea's vanity of mind: "You can scarcely be ignorant," he says—and the interruption in the statement is ironic—"that you know the world"; and he congratulates the auctioneer on his "reputation for that knowledge" (p. 64). Sapsea takes the compliment, and admits to having "enlarged [his] mind" (p. 65). "If I have not gone to foreign countries," he explains, "foreign countries have come to me." So vast is his experience of the world that he can "put [his] finger" upon clocks, cups and saucers, bamboo and sandalwood, and know them—or so he claims. Jasper congratulates him on this talent: "A very remarkable way, Mr. Sapsea, of acquiring knowledge of men and things" (p. 64). Jasper acquires his own knowledge, of course, in a similar way: but what is pompous stupidity in Sapsea is pathologically corrupt in Jasper. Everything Jasper knows has either its origin or its coloring—its meaning—inside Jasper's mind, and he cares for no other reality. When Sapsea congratulates himself on his "extensive knowledge of the world"—his model clock is from Paris, his teacups represent "Pekin, Nankin, and Canton"; his experience includes things Japanese, Egyptian, and "Esquimaux" (p. 64)—we must look comparatively at Jasper's world: the "cramped monotony of [his] existence" (p. 48) in Cloisterham contrasts with the mental visions he entertains of that "hoarde of Turkish robbers," the Sultan and his dancing girls, as he lies across a bed with a Chinaman and a Lascar at the Princess Puffer's (p. 37).

The chapter in which Jasper and Durdles visit the Cathedral by night begins with a conversation between Jasper, the Dean, and Sapsea. Jasper refers to Sapsea and his "knowledge of mankind" as the source of his interest in Durdles and exploring the Cathedral. Flattering Sapsea, Jasper refers to his ability "with a few skilful touches" to turn a "character . . . inside out" (p. 148). When Sapsea expresses his prejudice against Neville—for looking "Un-English"—Jasper "is truly sorry to hear [him] speak thus, for he knows right well that Mr. Sapsea never speaks without a meaning, and that he has a subtle trick of being right" (p. 180); when Neville is to be accused before Sapsea, Jasper declares for his pawn "that he place[s] his whole reliance, humanly speaking, on Mr. Sapsea's penetration" (p. 188).

Sapsea knows nothing; he is a pompous, prejudiced ass. But Jasper knows what he is doing. Though it may be that he only acts out killing Edwin in his opium dreams, Jasper's hypocritical use of Sapsea is evidence of his own indulged prejudices, and his catering to Sapsea's stupid egotism reveals Jasper's own wicked ego. Jasper looks at the world through jealous, self-tormenting eyes; he sees it only as he wants to see it, and in a mixture of dishonesty and delirious honesty sees its truth as what he wants that truth to be.

Neville and Helena have a remarkable "understanding" (p. 91) of each other, which comes naturally to them. Edwin and Rosa don't understand each other very well, as lovers, partly because they think only of themselves, not of one another. As friends, however, they quickly discover mutual sympathy, and in the "softening light" of this "gentle and forbearing feeling of each towards the other" their "relations" become "elevated into something more self-denying, honorable, affectionate, and true" (pp. 164–65). Edwin even learns to see "himself . . .

clearly, in a glass of [Rosa's] holding up," and understands
how he has "patronized her," and how such conduct is evidence that something has been "radically amiss" in their relationship (pp. 165–66). Rosa, he concludes, is "so much firmer
and wiser than he had supposed" (pp. 175–76).

The most interesting characters in their "knowing," however, are not the young people, but Grewgious, Crisparkle,
and Dick Datchery. Most of Dickens's novels focus on their
young people, for whom growing up and learning become
essentially the same thing. *Edwin Drood,* however, is more
particularly an *adult* novel, written for an audience which has
already grown up. Though it has four young people in it, and
they are all involved both in growing up and in learning how
to be wise, the primary focus is on a larger kind of knowing,
a comprehensive and comprehending kind of "watching" that
those who are grown up take on as their role, their duty.

Grewgious is a very deliberate man, yet self-effacing in his
manner. The first time we see him with Jasper, he "very knowingly [feels] his way round" him as he speaks (p. 119). In
talking to Rosa he professes himself to be a man of "no
imagination" (p. 140), with "not . . . a morsel of fancy" about
him (p. 141); "I never," he says, "to my knowledge, got within
ten thousand miles" of "what I understand to be poetry" (p.
142). At the end of this scene, however, he falls briefly into
a "wondering" mood (p. 146); and when he is needed, Grewgious can even "entertain a sort of fancy" (p. 212) concerning
Neville, and "have an idea" (p. 244) about evading Jasper's
watches.

Ideas don't come from nowhere, however; they aren't made
out of "miracles" either. Grewgious wants to keep Neville
"under his eye" in London, but the side of the building which
he happens to watch happens not to show him much. Because
"his eye [is] on the front of the house and not the back" (p.
216), he doesn't know about Tartar yet, who is introducing
himself to Neville at the rear of the house while Grewgious
wastes his watching on the front:

> But, Mr. Grewgious seeing nothing there, not even a light in the
> windows, his gaze wandered from the windows to the stars, as if
> he would read in them something hidden from him. Many of us

would, if we could; but none of us so much as know our letters in the stars yet—or seem likely to, in this state of existance—and few languages can be read until their alphabets are mastered. (216)

Once Tartar has introduced himself to the larger company of Neville's friends, Grewgious arranges the pieces of new information which this meeting gives him, and puts them together with what he wants—to foil Jasper's "watches"—and calls it an "idea." As he explains it, Crisparkle and Tartar comment that they "begin to understand," and finally, as Grewgious says, "we have all got the idea" (p. 245). And it hasn't come from nowhere, or from "looking at the stars." It comes from his finding out "what was hidden from him." The narrator's generalization about the likely limits to what we know "in this state of existence" is qualified by the acts of people like Grewgious. There is a great deal we can know, if we will set about to learn it.

The stars aren't alone in having special "languages" which hold but hide their wisdom. In the first chapter Jasper listens carefully, trying to make out words from the "mutterings" of the Princess and her other patrons, but is frustrated: their words are "unintelligible" (pp. 39–40). In the final chapter, the Princess tries to find out what Jasper's "incoherence" means, hoping to find "the secret of how to make [him] talk" (pp. 271–72). Deputy has a comic little language of his own, ranging from "kinfreederel" to "Widdy widdy wen" in its vocabulary; and Datchery has in his secret way of "keeping scores" with chalk-marks—another private language.

Neville is busy studying the difficult language of the law, under Crisparkle's tutelage. The chapter which ends with Grewgious contemplating the stars and the narrator warning us how hard to read their language is, begins with Crisparkle's using strong words on Neville's behalf against Honeythunder's abuse of language and his "platform resource" of twisting meanings (pp. 205–08). Crisparkle argues "with perfect command of himself" (p. 205) and with nothing of "self-assertion" (p. 206), devoting his aroused energies to an assertion of the simple things he knows to be true and the value and duty of friendship. Knowledge and friendship—what the mind can comprehend and what it touches—are very often one for Crisparkle, and their relationship is underscored by his habitual coupling of mental and bodily well-being. All four come together as he enters Neville's room in Staple Inn, and observes him at his studies:

> "How goes it, Neville?"
> "I am in good heart, Mr. Crisparkle, and working away."
> "I wish your eyes were not quite so large and not quite so bright," said the Minor Canon, slowly releasing the hand he had taken in his.
> "They brighten at the sight of you," returned Neville. (208)

In the manuscript,[7] Dickens creates Crisparkle's gesture of "slowly releasing the hand he has taken in his" interlinearly, having already written Neville's response to the Minor Canon's statement (Ms. 142). Together, the gesture and Neville's response make a perfect pair, as communication: Crisparkle's having held young Neville's hand is a gesture of affection, and it is answered by Neville's words of affection. Earlier, Crisparkle has spoken to Neville and Helena of "the wisdom of Love," and has told them that "it was the highest wisdom ever known upon this earth" (p. 130).

Crisparkle is curiously certain of "the wisdom of Love"— curiously so because the text which this world presents on the subject reads generally contrary to such a belief. Grewgious has been "born advanced in life" (p. 114), and is an "Angular bachelor" (p. 237) who has loved only "at a hopeless, speechless distance" (p. 146). Miss Twinkleton is a spinster, whose only acquaintance with love came in the person of "Foolish Mr. Porters" (p. 53); Mrs. Tisher is "a deferential widow with a weak back, a chronic sigh, and a suppressed voice" (p. 53), and Mrs. Billickin, though hardly deferential, is a widow (p. 253). Mr. Crisparkle lives alone with Mrs. Crisparkle— "mother, not wife"—her other six children all having died in infancy (p. 78). Neville and Helena have been raised by a "cruel brute" and "miserly wretch" of a stepfather (p. 88), and then by the perverse philanthropist Honeythunder. Sapsea had a "reverential wife" in Ethelinda (p. 67)—who was lucky enough to die early. Edwin's and Rosa's parent's are dead, and Edwin and Rosa can't manage to love each other, despite injunctions to do so. Deputy is an orphan, Durdles a "bachelor" who leads a "gypsy sort of life" (p. 68), and Datchery describes himself as "a single buffer getting through life upon his means" (p. 200). Tartar is a bachelor, too, and Jasper is unmarried.

But the world is capable of love and of loving, if it will grow wise: and that is the point of this novel. As friends, Edwin and Rosa establish "so serene an understanding" (p. 169) that we can be sure of their love. Helena and Neville love each other, and Helena and her brother both love Rosa. Edwin and Neville are both wise enough, by the novel's end, to love each other—if Edwin still lives. Crisparkle is vindicated, and there is justification, then, for the "brilliant morning" which "shines on the old city," and for the "changes of glorious light" and "songs of birds" and "scents . . . from the one great garden of the whole cultivated island in its yielding time" to "preach the Resurrection and the Life" (p. 278). The narrative voice proposes in nature a symbol of affirmation for this beautiful wisdom; spring speaks its high truth in nature's language, and we are shown, then, one last brief scene from the human world, to test if we are wise. The choir enters the Cathedral; the Choir Master, "musically fervid," "chants and sings" (p. 279). Along with the Princess Puffer, Deputy, and Dick Datchery, we look on: watching. The service ends, and Datchery goes home to his breakfast. Triumphant now in what he knows, he marks his score, and "falls to with an appetite" (p. 280).

NOTES

1. *Oxford English Dictionary*, volume P, p. 554.
2. This second light was an after-thought; the phrase "with no light but that of the fire" is added interlinearly in the manuscript (Ms. 102).
3. Given the general playfulness of the narrative voice, one might be tempted to find a pun connection from looking and watching and warning to Edwin's lost watch.
4. *Impressions and Comments* (London, 1920), p. 157.
5. *Wer:* man + *ald:* age. *Oxford English Dictionary*, volume W, p. 300.
6. Jasper doesn't mesmerize Rosa—or if he does, the significance of such is symbolic rather than straight or simple. Whichever way we read it, mesmerism isn't the point of the scene. Rosa is aware of Jasper's looking at her, and she knows what his looks mean. She is terrified of Jasper, not mesmerized by him: "I can't bear this!" she says. "I am frightened" (p. 92).
7. Manuscript in the Forster Collection at the Victoria and Albert Museum.

CHAPTER 9

"And thus ... everything comes to an end."

Dick Datchery "falls to with an appetite": this may seem to be a curious way to end a novel, but given the kind of novel it concludes there is really nothing at all odd about it. Given the way Dickens has created the novel, through the narrative voice, *Edwin Drood* must end in this or some similar way. Let me argue this point briefly, and that the novel is indeed ended —completed—with these last words, and I will have done.

First, however, let me say something about food, and what Datchery's "appetite" means. Like most of Dickens's other novels, *Edwin Drood* is full of eating. One of the first jokes in the novel is about food, and it is important in that it teaches us immediately something of how we must read to make sense of things. The Dean speaks to Crisparkle and Tope after vespers: "Our affections, however laudable, in this transitory world, should never master us; we should guide them, guide them." He continues, as proof against his own advice: "I find I am not disagreeably reminded of my dinner, by hearing my dinner-bell" (p.42). Edwin and Jasper sit down to dinner in the same chapter (p. 45), Jasper dines with Sapsea in chapter 4 (p. 71), and the Crisparkles have dinner guests in chapter 6 (pp. 86–87). The girls eat at Miss Twinkleton's (pp. 160, 171), and Mrs. Billickin carries on her wars with Miss Twinkleton over menus and meals (pp. 260, 262). Neville stops for breakfast as he leaves Cloisterham on Christmas Day (p. 184), and the Princess Puffer buys milk and bread as she waits for Jasper in London (p. 272). The occasion of the meeting between Neville and Edwin at the Gate House is dinner, and the clue Tartar gives Crisparkle is "What will you have for breakfast this morning? You are out of jam" (p. 243). And Durdles is always either eating or preparing to eat when we see him.

In terms of meaning and focus, the most significant eating in the novel is done by Grewgious and Datchery. With the exception of Durdles's munching and bolting and fearing indigestion, discussed above, all the rest of the eating in the novel is a part of the dramatic setting more than anything else. But Grewgious makes so much of food that we begin to see meaning in its appearance.[1] As soon as Edwin arrives at Staple Inn, Grewgious invites him to dine (p. 137); later, when Rosa arrives, he insists that she eat. "What did you take last?" he asks. "Was it breakfast, lunch, dinner, tea, or supper? And what will you take next? Shall it be breakfast, lunch, dinner, tea, or supper?" (p. 236). When he leaves her for the night, his last promise is that her "breakfast will be provided" for her (p. 241). Between these two scenes is the scene in which Grewgious watches Jasper disintegrate (pp. 190–92), after which he is asked to "take something" to eat with Jasper. Revolted by what he has seen, Grewgious declines the invitation: "I couldn't get a morsel down my throat," he replies (p. 193).

Eating is a social act as well as a nutritional necessity, and Grewgious treats it as such on the occasions when society is possible. Society isn't always possible, however, and Grewgious therefore eats his dinner alone in Furnival's Inn some "three hundred days in the year" (p. 135)—but this doesn't make Grewgious less socially conscious or discerning when the chance for society presents itself. Datchery, however, always dines alone. When he enters the novel, in chapter 18, he immediately orders his dinner, detailed as "fried sole, veal cutlet, and pint of sherry" (p. 217). When next we see him, in the final chapter, returning home and "sitting long over [his] supper of bread and cheese and salad and ale" (p. 278), he follows his meal with a "moderate stroke" of "scoring" on the cupboard door, and goes to bed (p. 278). The last we see of him, the next morning at breakfast, he marks his score and "falls to with an appetite" (p. 280). Eating is not a social act for Datchery—but it is connected with the social act of seeing and learning. Knowledge, for Dickens, is a social virtue—and Datchery's "appetite" is indicative of his social responsibility.

Earlier I called Datchery's way of keeping score with chalk-marks a private language. As it is a language, it makes Datchery a character something like Mortimer Lightwood, and suggests for his watching the same social significance that Mortimer's has. By watching—and learning—Mortimer assumes responsibility for the story of *Our Mutual Friend.* Dick Datchery—whoever he is—does the same thing in *Edwin Drood,* assuming responsibility for solving its "mystery." As an unknown character—someone in disguise, named "Dick" —he assumes that responsibility for us, and in that way becomes a social character. His "appetite" at the end contrasts with Grewgious's disgusted inability to eat after he sees Jasper's evil, and with Durdles's fear that what he has seen in Jasper's face will cause him indigestion; it contrasts also with Jasper's eating "without appetite" (p. 266) just before his last visit to the Princess Puffer's den. Datchery's "appetite" comes from exultation: and his exultation comes from what he knows. That he "falls to with an appetite" is like what Mortimer does in the last line of *Our Mutual Friend,* as he "fares to the Temple, gaily" (p. 892). Datchery has put together all that he has seen, and is satisfied with the whole of what he knows. The world this morning is "brilliant" and "beautiful" and "warm," and "the Resurrection and the Life" are natural again. With what he knows—and knowing is the natural responsibility of man, for Dickens—Datchery can join the world in its celebration.

If this strange novel is to succeed, we must be able to join the world with Datchery at its end. In this farewell novel, Dickens goes to remarkable extremes to teach us how to learn what we need to learn. In *David Copperfield* the lesson he teaches with David's life is the double one of reflection and comprehension; in this last novel the emphasis is more particularly on comprehension. But in *Edwin Drood* we aren't asked simply to learn what the novel tells us; if we try that we will get confused by the ways the narrative voice plays and makes jokes in the middle of what seems to be a murder mystery. Rather than learn what we are told, we have to watch the patterning of details and the kinds of comments the narrator makes about them, so that we may come to see the world of the novel as the narrator sees it. This time Dickens is out to teach us not just what he knows but how to know it. If *David Copperfield* is David's act of remembering or recollecting his life and that of the world around him, into meaning, *Edwin Drood* is a partial mimicking of that act and an invitation to us to join in the creative experience and expression of such meaning. If *David Copperfield* is Dickens's novel, written in a way for himself as an artist, *Edwin Drood* is in a very special way our novel, as audience—and *we* are "in" its world, "to be of it."

The opening paragraphs set the theme for *The Mystery of Edwin Drood.* How can this be? And what does it mean? In the second chapter the narrator does his version of the nutcracker suite as a variation on the more traditional narrative mode. In the third he introduces in one sentence a marvellously complex simile which touches upon almost everything of importance in the whole novel. The sentence is supposedly about the two separate states of Miss Twinkleton's existence—the public or "scholastic" state and the private or personal one:

> As, in some cases of drunkenness, and in others of animal magnetism, there are two states of consciousness which never clash, but each of which pursues its separate course as though it were continuous instead of broken (thus, if I hide my watch when I am drunk, I must be drunk again before I can remember where), so Miss Twinkleton has two distinct and separate phases of being. (53)

The allusions to "drunkenness" and "animal magnetism" are false leads, at best; the parenthetical example of the lost watch is more interesting and closer to the point. But what is most significant is the description of the "two states of consciousness . . . each of which pursues its separate course." All of this material is contained in what pretends to be the subordinate clause of the sentence; Miss Twinkleton's "two distinct and separate phases of being" are supposedly the focus of the statement. The form of the sentence suggests, thus, that there are larger connections and larger meanings in seemingly discrete and simple facts of circumstances.

But we have to be careful. Miss Twinkleton doesn't get drunk, or hide her watch; and her "phases of being" are a fiction designed to serve a purpose. In her private state, the "sprightly Miss Twinkleton whom the young ladies have never seen" is quite different from her professional self, on view all day as an example of propriety in the school. In her private state she is—among other things—a gossip; but in her "scholastic state of existence" Miss Twinkleton "has no knowledge whatever" of "the tenderer scandal of Cloisterham" (p. 53). Her "scholastic state" is thus a sham—and the point of the simile, then, is in the representation of hypocrisy, not in the idea of "separate states of being." We are not to use the narrator's odd example—"if I hide my watch when I am drunk, I must be drunk again before I can remember where" —as an excuse to go looking for Edwin's missing watch, or to start suspecting Durdles of murder because he gets drunk. Rather, we must use the meaning of the simile derivable from its application to Miss Twinkleton. Then, when we refer the simile to other characters in other situations, as the "hide my watch" example invites us to, we discover that though Jasper indulges in dreams of violence under the influence of opium, he is just as violent in his other "state"—and still more evil because false.

Making connections—"making nets," David would say—is what a work of art is all about, and the narrative voice invites us to make such throughout this novel. Scenes and chapters exist as complex units of meaning, and must be read as such. The most telling of these are chapters 10 and 12.

Chapter 10 opens with the remark that "women have a curious power of divining the characters of men," which introduces "the fair diviner" Mrs. Crisparkle and her "unfair" divination concerning Neville (p. 120). When the Minor Canon falls into "a little reverie" (p. 122) and silently pursues a serious line of "thought" for some minutes, his mother sets about finding a remedy for the malady. She makes haste, we are told, "to the dining-room closet, to produce from it the support embodied in a glass of Constantia and a home-made biscuit" (p. 123). But it is two full pages before her son drinks his dose of Constantia; a "meander" intervenes, larger than any David ever allows himself, in which the contents of first the dining-room closet (p. 123) and then the "medicinal herb-closet" (p. 124) are detailed, item by item. Like David's mean-derings, of course, these descriptions are not really digressions. Again, as in *David Copperfield,* everything is to the point. Because this is the world—the real world—everything, Dickens insists, must combine into meaning.

The second paragraph of the roll-call of the closets in Mi-nor Canon Corner concludes with the notation that Crispar-kle regularly takes his medicine to please his mother—and then goes out, "as confident of the sweetening powers of Cloisterham Weir and a wholesome mind, as Lady Macbeth was hopeless of those of all the seas that roll" (p. 124). We have no reason to connect Crisparkle with Lady Macbeth—even negatively—in guilt or hopelessness, so the allusion seems irrelevant.

In the middle of the chapter Crisparkle talks with Neville and Helena. Despite Mrs. Crisparkle's divination of his char-acter, Neville makes himself agreeable to us by his insistent honesty, and convinces us of his goodness. When Crisparkle stops at Jasper's Gate House to report to him Neville's apology for his part in the angry scene with Edwin, he wakes the Choir Master from "an indigestive after-dinner sleep" (p. 130).[2] Jasper's face assumes a "perplexed and perplexing expression" when Crisparkle explains his purpose in calling, and seems to the puzzled Minor Canon "to denote (which could hardly be) some close internal calculation." Then sud-denly "the perplexed and perplexing look vanishe[s]"—and the innocent Crisparkle is "delighted by the swiftness and completeness of his success" (p. 131) on Neville's behalf. Jasper tells him that he will make of this assurance for Neville "an antidote" to his "black humors" (p. 132), and Crisparkle responds encouragingly, "Try the antidote" (p. 133).

The form of the whole should now be clear, and with the form its meaning. The chapter opens with Mrs. Crisparkle's unreasonable condemnation of Neville, and then lets Neville himself persuade us of his essential goodness. Two pages full of condiments and remedies are presented to us early in the chapter, and Mrs. Crisparkle administers a dose of one to her son; at the end of the chapter Jasper suddenly and unexpect-

edly announces that he will take "an antidote" to dispel his
"black humors." The narrative hint that Jasper is engaged in
"some close internal calculation" suggests to us that he is
lying to Crisparkle in accepting the Minor Canon's pledge for
Neville; more importantly, the idea of an "antidote" takes us
back to the herb-closet. The remark there about Lady
Macbeth will now make sense. Crisparkle doesn't need drugs
to restore his health: he is "as confident in the sweetening
powers of Cloisterham Weir and a wholesome mind, as Lady
Macbeth was hopeless of those of all the seas that roll." Crisparkle is clean in mind and body—naturally; but Jasper, like
Lady Macbeth, can't cleanse his mind, because he is already
guilty *in* his mind.

Chapter 12 is organized similarly. It begins with Sapsea as
he "takes an airing in the Cathedral Close and thereabout" (p.
147), and ends with Deputy appearing in the same place,
having "come out for [his] 'elth" (p. 160). Sapsea is on the
lookout for "a stranger coming from the churchyard" (p.
147), but instead meets Jasper, the Dean, and Tope. Their
conversation together is but a prelude; later in the evening
Jasper and Durdles "are to make a moonlight hole-and-cor-
ner exploration of the Cathedral" (p. 149), for reasons which
the narrator professes not to understand:

> Surely an unaccountable sort of expedition! That Durdles him-
> self . . . should be stealing forth to climb, and dive, and wander,
> without an object, is nothing extraordinary; but that the Choir
> Master or any one else should hold it worth his while to be with
> him . . . is another affair. Surely an unaccountable sort of expedi-
> tion, therefore! (151)

The effect of this paragraph, of course, is to tell us that the
expedition must be accountable, just as there being "no out-
ward reason" for Jasper's going "so softly" out tonight makes
clear the answer to the narrator's question, "Can there be any
sympathetic reason crouching darkly within him?" (p. 151).
Jasper has told the Dean that his interest in the Cathedral is
the result of mere "whim" and "curiosity" (p. 148); but the
narrator suggests strongly that there must be a more serious
reason for "the Choir Master or any one else" to undertake

such an expedition as this, and he urges us to watch for it.

The next element of the chapter involves Jasper's watching Neville "as though his eye were at the trigger of a loaded rifle," and Durdles's distressed discovery of the "destructive power . . . expressed in [Jasper's] face" (p. 152). Then comes a long paragraph about ghosts. But there are no ghosts here: "when Mr. Jasper and Durdles pause to glance around them, before descending into the crypt . . . the whole expanse of moonlight in their view is utterly deserted" (p. 154). Durdles soon tells Jasper, however, of having fallen asleep in this place on "the last Christmas Eve," and of having been awakened by a ghost, or rather "the ghost of a cry" (p. 155). The two of them explore the Cathedral, going up the tower and out onto the roof, and then back down into the crypt "with the intent of issuing forth as they entered" (p. 157). It is at this point that Durdles, drugged by Jasper, falls asleep: "and in his sleep he dreams a dream"—which "is not much of a dream, considering the vast extent of the domains of dreamland," but is rather "remarkable for being . . . unusually real" (p. 157).

Durdles's "dream" is that Jasper takes the key from his hand, and leaves him alone for some time—which is exactly what has happened. Because this novel is about psychological states and the realities of the mind, this representation of a "dream" that is "real" must reflect on other dreams, and in so doing suggest their potential for reality. Thus Durdles's dream of "the ghost of a cry" last Christmas Eve is not just a dream; it may be fulfilled this Christmas Eve—if Jasper has his way. And Jasper's dream of violence, with which the novel began, is not just a dream, either: whether or not he actually commits his crime, that dream is Jasper's reality, over and over and always.

At the end of the chapter, Durdles and Jasper emerge from the crypt at last, and Deputy—happening to be there—sees them. He gives his usual "warning" cry, and begins to stone Durdles. Jasper, monomaniacal and guilty, thinks Deputy has been watching him: his reality usurps all others.

When we look at the whole chapter, now, we see that the expedition in the Cathedral which Jasper told the Dean was but a "whim" of his was hardly that at all, and hardly even just a purposeful reconnoitering. In his mind, Jasper has accomplished tonight whatever evil he means to accomplish in the Cathedral on Christmas Eve. Durdles's dream from last year and his reality-matching dream this night tell us all we need to know about Jasper's midnight adventures there, and the scene won't be repeated. Though Jasper has undertaken this expedition presumably to plan for the future, planning crosses over into enactment in the obsessed mind—and we know what he has done!

The narrator of *Edwin Drood* regularly expects us to make connections like these, and draw meaning from them. If we don't, we end up with a novel full of irrelevancies and distractions, a story made up of the uncollectable fragments of an unfinished and impossible "mystery." There is no mystery, however, if we read well; and all the pieces come together, alive with meaning. But we have to work hard: the narrator doesn't make it easy for us. We have to be ready to read about London's sparrows in relation to Cloisterham's rooks, and accept a seemingly irrelevant interpolated paragraph[3] on London street-music (p. 235). We have to read all about Bazzard and his tragedy twice from Grewgious, and listen to Miss Twinkleton ramble inconclusively about that Spartan general she had better have forgotten. And we have to know why all of these details are here, and what they mean.

The narrator persists, also, in taking nothing too seriously, and everywhere intruding his wry and often facetious attitude toward this world. Edwin calls Rosa "Rosa dear"—and the narrator mimics him (p. 53). Because Mrs. Billikin hides her sex behind the protection of a genderless doorplate, the narrator always refers to her playfully as "the Billikin"—and finally calls her simply "the B" (p. 259). The inscription over the door where Grewgious lives in Staple Inn reads "P J T 1747"—which the narrator variously elaborates as "Perhaps John Thomas" or "Perhaps Joe Tyler" (p. 134), "Pretty Jolly Too" (p. 140), and "Possibly Jabbered Thus" (p. 146).[4] There are a thousand more small jokes—twists, puns, teases, asides—in the narrative sections of the novel. For the most part they don't have any particular or individual meaning, and they won't come together as necessary to the story being told.

They are, however, an essential part of the sense of the novel: they tell us how the narrator sees the story, and they invite us to try to view it in the same way.

But we can't quite do that. Dickens is writing this last novel from a perspective we can't manage yet. He is about to leave this world—there are clues to that all through the novel—and he is leaving it "gaily." We are still in it, however, and still have to struggle to find both its meaning and our happiness—and to find that those two are finally one, and the same. In *David Copperfield* we watched in awe as David, the artist, achieved that comprehension of the world that we call first art and then life. In *Our Mutual Friend* Dickens took us with him and his characters, and taught us from a closer perspective what tragedy is and how glorious its achievement is. In *Edwin Drood,* however, nothing is solved or resolved when the novel ends: when it is finished. We are left in the living world: "in it, to be of it."

Jasper begins *Edwin Drood* with an unfinished dream (p. 37). Edwin's "unfinished picture" of Rosa hangs over the chimneypiece in the Gate House (p. 43). Mrs Sapsea always addresses her husband in "unfinished terms" (p. 66). Nature doesn't bother to "finish off" Grewgious's face (p. 110). Durdles lives in "a house that was never finished" (pp. 68, 151), and seems once about to fall into an "unfinished" tomb (p. 77). These things are unfinished—not the novel they are in. I know, of course, that Dickens planned twelve monthly numbers for *Edwin Drood*, but wrote only six, and that he even wrote down the Roman numeral for a chapter 23 which he didn't live to write. But he usually made notes for each chapter and for the whole monthly part—and he made none for either of the chapters he wrote for the final part of *Edwin Drood*, and none for that final part itself. This seems to me curious—especially when I look at how much ground is covered in that final chapter, "The Dawn Again." Individual chapters in this novel have so often been carefully constructed units—and this last long one seems to be designed to tie up everything in the whole novel!

More curious, however, are an odd set of seemingly reflexive references to death in the novel. Individually they mean nothing; collectively, however, they seem to me to suggest in Dickens a chosen, more subjective awareness of death than we have seen in any of his other novels.

When Jasper goes to Durdles's "unfinished house" to pick him up for their expedition to the Cathedral, the narrator sees metaphorically "two skeleton journeymen . . . cutting out the gravestones of the next two people to die in Cloisterham." Then he muses, with an odd and teasing playfulness: "Likely enough, the two think little of that now, being alive, and perhaps merry. Curious, to make a guess at the two;—or say at one of the two!" (p. 151). We are supposed to guess Edwin for the one, of course. Who would we guess for the other?

When Jasper and Durdles go to the top of the Cathedral tower, and "look down on Cloisterham," they look at three aspects of it: "its ruined habitations and sanctuaries of the dead," "its moss-softened . . . houses of the living," and "its river winding down from the mist on the horizon, as though that were its source, and already heaving with a restless knowledge of its approach towards the sea" (156). The Victorians were fond of the river as a metaphor for life, and of going out to sea as meaning death; Dickens uses the image more than once in other novels. The self-conscious river here stands out in its self-consciousness, and seems symbolic in its "heaving with a restless knowledge" of its approaching end.

At the beginning of chapter 14, on Christmas Eve, the streets of Cloisterham are filled with "strange faces" and "other faces, half strange and half fantastic," drawn back to the city "from the outer world." Others like them, "in their dying hours afar off," have seemed to return to Cloisterham "when the circle of their lives was very nearly traced, and the beginning and the end were drawing close together" (pp. 170–71). As an introduction to a chapter entitled "When Shall These Three Meet Again," this is all rather melodramatic, though it does have several minor thematic connections with the novel as a whole. If we recognize, however, that —as Carlyle says—all speech is first autobiographical and then about its external subject, this brief meditation on the completion of life is understandable in a much more profound way. It is Dickens's commentary on making meaning out of life in this world.

When Dick Datchery arrives at Cloisterham, he speaks of his "inclination to end [his] days in the city" (p. 221). From his description as "a white-haired personage with black eyebrows" (p. 216) we don't expect him to be old—particularly since the narrator teases us so much with the possibility that the white hair is a wig. So why should he think of dying? In the manuscript, Dickens originally had Datchery speak of his "inclination towards the city" (Ms. 149); this is revised interlinearly, so that his "inclination" is towards death; "to end [his] days in the city." Why?

Grewgious is another character who has long since "settled down . . . for the rest of his life" (p. 135) in London. In some ways, Grewgious is the most interesting character in *Edwin Drood.* He is the main adult, and as guardian, watcher, and knower he is one of the most important characters. He and Dick Datchery are seemingly Dickens's characters here—that is why, I presume, Datchery is named Dick—in the same way that Mortimer is his character in *Our Mutual Friend.* At the end of the novel, Datchery replaces Grewgious: or at least Datchery watches in Cloisterham, while Grewgious watches in London.

When we first meet Grewgious in his London chambers, at Staple Inn, one curious detail stands out: he lives in terror "of dying suddenly, and leaving one fact or one figure with any incompleteness or obscurity attached to it" (p. 135). This little bit of information stands out in the context of the various seemingly unfocused notes and comments about death; more, in a novel which is supposedly "unfinished," left incomplete at the author's death, a character who lives in "apprehension of dying suddenly" and leaving "incompleteness and obscurity" behind him is either a fantastically coincidental creation or a significantly intentional one. I opt for the latter: and would propose that what the narrator says about Grewgious is an autobiographical clue, in a way.[5]

Edwin Drood has always seemed to me a finished novel, ever since the first time I read it. It seemed to me from the beginning a novel about Jasper, not about Drood. The more I read it now—and the more I understand about Jasper—the more it seems to be about understanding Jasper, or just about understanding. It seems to me finally a novel that proposes to teach me how to understand the world. Dickens tried this kind of novel first in *David Copperfield,* and tried it again in a slightly different way in *Our Mutual Friend.* David's novel is his test—for himself—of whether he has learned to understand the world, and can thus become "the hero of [his] own life" (p. 49). At the end of *Our Mutual Friend,* Bella keeps asking to be "tested," and Mortimer's last excursion into Society is also a sort of test, self-administered. In *Edwin Drood,* Dickens gives us the test: gives it to us as a gift, as his last, best gift, in fact.

At the end of *David Copperfield,* David left the world behind him—for us. At the end of *Our Mutual Friend,* Dickens left Mortimer in the world, and the world unchanged; but he left Mortimer capable of surviving in that world, by knowing it. At the end of *Edwin Drood,* Dickens leaves us in the world: in the living world, with nothing solved or resolved. Its solution and resolution are up to us. Knowing it is all up to us—if we would be the heroes of our lives!

What an exhilarating way to finish: the artist gives us the richness of the world, alive, with the encouragement which will let us learn it. That's the happiest ending possible—and I think Dickens knew it.

NOTES

1. The "closet" in Grewgious's room "usually containing something good to drink" (p. 135) should remind us of the "closet" full of good things to eat and the "herb-closet" at Minor Canon Corner, introduced in the previous chapter.
2. The narrator lapses momentarily into simple conventional narration at this point. Crisparkle looks in at Jasper's door, and the narrator says, "Long afterwards he had cause to remember how Jasper sprang from the couch in a delirious state between sleeping and waking, crying out: 'What is the matter? Who did it?' " (p. 130).
3. Added overleaf in the manuscript (Ms. 158).
4. Dickens's tricks with P J T remind this reader of Joyce's similar tricks with H C E in *Finnegan's Wake.*
5. An interesting and related story is told by Henry Fielding Dickens, of an autobiographical detail which Dickens slipped into a game the family were playing at Christmas in 1869: "We had been playing a game that

evening known as 'The Memory Game,' in which, after a while, my father joined, throwing all his energy into it, as he always did in anything he put his hand to. One of the party started by giving a name, such as, for instance, Napoleon. The next person had to repeat this and add something of his own, such as Napoleon, Blackbeetle, and so on . . . My father, after many turns, had successfully gone through the long string of words, and finished up with his own contribution, 'Warren's Blacking, 30, Strand.' He gave this with an odd twinkle in his eye and a strange inflection in his voice which forcibly arrested my attention and left a vivid impression on my mind for some time afterwards. Why, I could not, for the life of me, understand. When, however, his tragic history appeared in Forster's Life, this game at Christmas, 1869, flashed across my mind with extraordinary force, and the mystery was explained." *Memories of My Father* (1928), pp. 23–23.

Index